SOUTHEAST ASIA
AND CHINA

Other Titles in This Series

Westview Special Studies on South and Southeast Asia

Southeast Asia and China: The End of Containment
Edwin W. Martin

Since the end of the war in Vietnam and the withdrawal of the American presence there, a marked realignment of power has taken place in Southeast Asia. The old rivalry between China and the United States has become a relationship of cautious rapprochement, while Sino–Soviet competition has been intensified by China's fear that the USSR will move to fill the power vacuum created by the U.S. departure.

The United States no longer perceives a friendly Sino-Southeast Asian relationship to be as much of a danger to its security interests as it once did, but how that relationship develops remains of considerable importance to this country. In this book, Edwin Martin examines some of the principal factors in China's current relations with the Southeast Asian countries—China's domestic policies, Peking-oriented insurgency in Southeast Asian countries, the Overseas Chinese, trade considerations, the policies of third powers—and concludes that the newly emergent nationalism in Southeast Asia, coupled with Sino–Soviet rivalry, indeed diminishes the threat posed by a Communist Indochina and calls for a U.S. policy of encouraging stable relations in the area, both among the countries themselves and between them and the PRC. He asserts that a four-way balance of power—involving the United States, the USSR, the PRC, and Japan—will prevent a power vacuum in the area and will allow the Southeast Asian countries to develop their own strengths, both political and economic. It is thus to the advantage of the United States to encourage all steps toward regional cooperation; U.S. policy, Professor Martin concludes, should neither abandon Southeast Asia, nor attempt to dictate to it.

Edwin W. Martin is currently Distinguished Professor of Diplomacy at Hiram College, Hiram, Ohio. A U.S. Foreign Service officer for over thirty years, his wide-ranging experience includes posts as ambassador to Burma, consul general in Hong Kong, minister-counselor at the U.S. Embassy in Ankara, and political advisor to CINCPAC, Honolulu. Professor Martin has degrees from Oberlin College and the Fletcher School of Law and Diplomacy and has studied at Yale University and the National War College.

SOUTHEAST ASIA AND CHINA

The End of Containment

Edwin W. Martin

Prepared for the Center for Strategic
and International Studies, Georgetown University

Westview Press
Boulder, Colorado

73140

Westview Special Studies on South and Southeast Asia

Copyright © 1977 by The Center for Strategic and International Studies, Georgetown University

Published 1977 in the United States of America by
  Westview Press, Inc.
  1898 Flatiron Court
  Boulder, Colorado 80301
  Frederick A. Praeger, Publisher and Editorial Director

Library of Congress Cataloging in Publication Data
Martin, Edwin W.
  Southeast Asia and China

  Includes bibliographical references.
1. Asia, Southeast—Foreign relations—China. 2. China—Foreign relations—
Asia, Southeast. 4. United States—Foreign relations—Asia, Southeast. I. Title.
DS518.15.M37   327.59'051   76-53510
ISBN 0-89158-219-3

Printed and bound in the United States of America

Contents

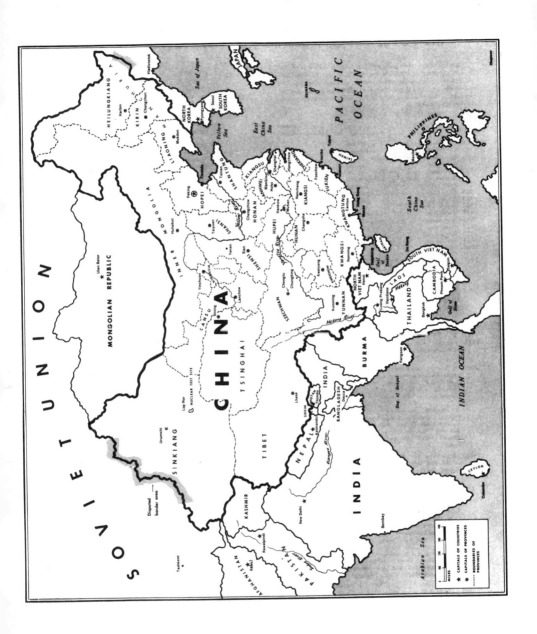

Foreword

Attitudes in the United States toward Southeast Asia have been equivocal since the decisive defeat suffered by South Vietnam at the hands of the Communist political leaders and armies of North Vietnam. The speedy reunification of Vietnam under the control of Hanoi marked the end of an era in U.S. strategy with a resounding disaster. It is not clear whether the People's Republic of China (PRC) or the Soviet Union won vicariously in Hanoi's triumph, but it is plain fact that U.S. hopes and efforts were frustrated.

Ambassador Edwin W. Martin, recently retired from the Foreign Service of the United States, has closely observed the unfolding of events in Southeast Asia. He has served in many diplomatic posts in Asia, ending his career with a tour in the 1970s as ambassador to Burma. He is exceptionally well qualified to comment on what happened in Vietnam and nearby states in recent years, on the PRC's policies toward the smaller states on its southern border, and on prospects for this region in the future.

Ambassador Martin concludes that a radical realignment of power relationships has taken place in Southeast Asia, where PRC-Soviet rivalry for strategic influence has become intense. He believes stability in the area depends on the formulation of new policies encouraging the regional development of economic resources within the framework of a four-way balance of power involving the United States, the Soviet Union, the PRC, and Japan.

Whatever the solution to the problem of Southeast Asia and its relations with the PRC, it is time for Americans to reformulate a meaningful diplomatic and strategic policy for the area. The Georgetown University Center for Strategic and International Studies is pleased to be able to sponsor Ambassador Martin's exceptionally thoughtful analysis of the problem based on his own long experience and study.

Ray S. Cline
Director of Studies
Georgetown University Center for
Strategic and International Studies

Introduction

For nearly two decades after the close of the Korean War in 1953, the United States perceived the People's Republic of China (PRC) as a serious threat to Southeast Asia, and American policy toward Southeast Asia was shaped by this perception. Typical of the American view during this period was the statement by President Kennedy in a television interview on September 9, 1963: "The fact of the matter is that with the assistance of the United States and SEATO, Southeast Asia and indeed all of Asia has been maintained independent against a powerful force, the Chinese Communists."[1]

By the mid-1970s, however, the situation had changed radically. The United States had all but abandoned its containment policy and viewed with equanimity the establishment of diplomatic relations between its Southeast Asian

allies, the Philippines and Thailand, and the PRC. Moreover, "in view of changing circumstances," that instrument
of containment, the Southeast Asia Treaty Organization
(SEATO), was being "phased out."[2] SEATO's last international exercise ended on February 20, 1976. Significantly,
it was a civil rather than a military exercise—building roads
and other facilities for Philippine communities.[3]

Today Sino-Soviet rivalry overshadows Sino-American
rivalry in Southeast Asia. Whereas the United States once
warned Thailand and other Southeast Asian countries
against the threat from the PRC, now the PRC warns them
against the threat from the Soviet Union. Thus Chinese Vice
Premier Teng Hsiao-ping, speaking at a welcoming banquet for Thai Prime Minister Kukrit Pramoj in Peking on
June 30, 1975, declared that following the "inevitable defeat" and withdrawal from Indochina of one superpower,
"the other superpower with wild ambitions has extended its
tentacles far and wide. It insatiably seeks new military bases
in Asia and sends its naval vessels to ply the Indian and west
Pacific oceans, posing a menacing threat to the peace and
security of Southeast Asian countries."[4]

While the United States no longer perceives the danger to
its security interests in the Sino-Southeast Asian relationship that it once did, nevertheless, how that relationship
develops in the coming years remains of considerable importance to this country. It is the purpose of this brief study to
examine some of the principal influencing factors—e.g.,
China's domestic policies, Peking-oriented insurgency,
Overseas Chinese, trade, and the policies of third powers—to
try to determine how Sino-Southeast Asian relations are
likely to develop over the next few years and to suggest some
implications for American policy.

Before proceeding with such an examination, however, it
may be helpful to draw attention to the special dimension

imparted by geography to the Sino-Southeast Asian relationship. China's propinquity is a significant fact which Southeast Asian countries must reckon with. China will not go away, and Peking does not hesitate to make political capital out of its immovable presence in the area. I recall, for example, that when I was living in Burma in 1950-1951, pro-Peking elements in the local Chinese community used to harp on the theme that while the influence of other powers might wax and wane, China's would always be present, and Peking would not forget who had been friend or foe. This line was designed primarily to influence the political behavior of Overseas Chinese in Burma, but it also had implications for the Burmese. Though other Southeast Asian countries may be less exposed to China's power than Burma, none is far enough away to ignore its potential.

Yet despite their propinquity, with the exception of Vietnam none of the countries of Southeast Asia has been effectively ruled by China for any length of time. The sending of tribute to Peking by some Southeast Asian countries in past centuries did not mean that they acknowledged Chinese sovereignty over them. Whatever the Chinese view of this practice may have been, it was for the Southeast Asians partly a form of trade and partly a matter of keeping a powerful neighbor happy. As an American historian has put it, "the small maritime states of Southeast Asia did no more than opportunistically acknowledge the Chinese definition of the world order in the interest of furthering their trade with the mainland."[5] Thus while there may be a tradition of accommodating to China among the Southeast Asian nations, there is none of subservience to Chinese domination.

Nevertheless, for China, propinquity gives Southeast Asia special strategic significance. If, for example, there had been an American ground invasion of North Vietnam there would have been a very high risk of a Chinese countermove.

Indeed, Chinese Foreign Minister Ch'en Yi is reported to have made an explicit statement along these lines.[6] As it was, Peking reacted to the American bombing of North Vietnam by sending tens of thousands of engineering troops into that country to repair roads, railroads, and bridges. In 1966 American officials estimated Chinese troop strength in North Vietnam at 50,000.[7]

This and other Chinese military assistance to North Vietnam was not rendered solely because of the PRC's concern for the defense of its borders. Peking never disguised its support of North Vietnam's goal of "liberating" South Vietnam and of Hanoi's use of force to achieve this end. There is no hard evidence, however, that Peking ever engaged its own military forces in the "liberation" of South Vietnam or intended to do so. In other words, there is an important distinction between the risks and costs the PRC will assume to support revolutionary wars and those it will incur to ward off a threat to its borders.

It is significant that the only other Southeast Asian countries where Peking has deployed its own armed forces are the only two besides North Vietnam having common borders with China, i.e., Laos and Burma. The PRC constructed a network of roads in northern Laos, using engineer units of the Chinese People's Liberation Army (PLA), and protected them with antiaircraft units. Although the government of Laos in 1962 apparently requested the PRC to build roads in this area, Peking subsequently greatly expanded the project to a point where by no stretch of the imagination could it be said that it had been carried out for the benefit of the Vientiane government. By 1975 it was estimated that the PLA had "carved more than 400 miles of strategic mountain highway south from China's Yunnan Province towards the sensitive Laos-Thailand border" and that 14,000 to 15,000 PLA troops were involved in building and guarding these roads.[8] While it has been widely speculated that the purpose of this construction was to facilitate Chinese logistical support of Communist insurgents in northern Thailand,[9] it is more likely that its principal purpose was to strengthen the PRC's defenses in the China-Laos-Burma border region and signal Peking's intention to react beyond its borders if hostile forces approached too closely.[10] In fact, Ch'en Yi's warning, mentioned above, applied to Laos as well as to North Vietnam.

The PRC has also moved in recent years to strengthen its borders with Burma. Thanks to direct Chinese support, including some military manpower, the Burmese Communist Party (BCP) insurgents were able to "liberate" thousands of square miles of Burmese territory along the China border in 1971-73.[11] The BCP's occupation of this territory gives China indirect control of substantial portions of the Burmese side of the China-Burma border.

PRC military involvement in Burma is less readily explained in terms of border security than are its road-building activities in Laos. Unlike Laos, Burma harbored no foreign forces and it was in no way embroiled in the Vietnam war. The fact that the BCP's major drive in eastern Burma began after the PRC's state relations with Burma had returned to normal and on the heels of Prime Minister Ne Win's August 1971 visit to China makes it even harder to understand Chinese involvement. The most plausible explanation seems to be that it represented a reaction to the Bangladesh war. Peking apparently saw India's invasion of East Pakistan within three months of the signing of a treaty between India and the Soviet Union as a dangerous expansion of Soviet influence on the western approaches to Burma,[12] and perhaps as the prelude to further moves in its direction.

In sum, despite the PRC's claims that it has had no troops on foreign soil, PLA units have been deployed in both North

Vietnam and Laos, while very small but significant numbers of Chinese military personnel have participated directly in BCP insurgency operations in eastern Burma. However, these military deployments in the three Southeast Asian states contiguous to China probably indicate Peking's concern for the security of its borders and its intention to react if hostile forces should approach too closely, rather than a policy of using the PLA to aid revolutionary wars in Southeast Asia. Nevertheless, propinquity gives China a potential for intervention in support of its security or ideological interests in Southeast Asia which it does not possess, for example, in Africa or Latin America.

1
Chinese Internal Developments

Relations between China and her Southeast Asian neighbors have been significantly affected by internal developments within individual nations. The Indonesian Communist Party's (PKI) attempted coup d'état of September 30, 1965, provides a dramatic example. The PKI's abortive coup resulted in the strongly anti-Communist Indonesian army's coming to power and in the eventual complete rupture of Sino-Indonesian relations, which for several years had been growing steadily closer. Other examples could also be given of domestic events in Southeast Asian countries which significantly affected their relations with the PRC, such as the ouster of Prince Sihanouk by the Cambodian National Assembly in March 1970. But such developments do not have as much significance for Sino–Southeast Asian relations as a whole as do China's internal affairs. Thus, only the impact of Chinese domestic developments on these relations will be considered here.

Prior to World War II there were no state relations between China and the countries of Southeast Asia. All of the latter but Thailand were colonies of one or another of the Western powers and as such had been deprived of the capacity to enter into diplomatic relations with other countries. Although Thailand was an independent state, it had deliberately refrained from establishing diplomatic relations with China, apparently because it feared the influence which a Chinese embassy might wield on the Overseas Chinese.

After World War II and before the establishment of the PRC on October 1, 1949, Thailand, the Philippines, and Burma (the latter two having achieved independence) entered into diplomatic relations with the Republic of China. Burma soon recognized the new government of the People's Republic (in December 1949), but Thailand and the Philippines did not do so until 1975, continuing their diplomatic relations with the government of the Republic of China for some twenty-five years after it moved to Taipei. Since 1975 no Southeast Asian government has had diplomatic relations with the government in Taipei; all but Indonesia and Singapore now maintain relations with Peking.

Since its establishment, the PRC has changed the direction and emphasis of its foreign policy several times. These changes have often reflected trends in domestic policy as well as the changing international environment. Broadly speaking, when revolutionary ideology has played a relatively strong role in the PRC's internal affairs, this has been reflected in a greater emphasis on the ideological aspects of the PRC's relations with other countries. Three such periods are especially significant: approximately the first four years of the PRC's existence; the period of the Great Leap Forward in the late 1950s; and that of the Great Proletarian Cultural

Revolution in the latter half of the 1960s.

In the PRC's early years, China's new Communist rulers needed above all to consolidate their revolutionary victory. This meant rooting out all vestiges of what they regarded as colonialist and imperialist, i.e., Western, influence. Moreover, flushed with the success of their own revolutionary struggle at home, they not unnaturally emphasized revolutionary objectives in their foreign relations. In this period, as one sinologist has put it, the "revolutionary component in the PRC's foreign policy was "overt and intense."[13]

Peking's concern with consolidating the revolution in China and promoting it abroad was symbolized by its posture of "lean to one side" in international affairs, which at that time meant leaning to the side of the Soviet Union. The concrete expression of this policy was the signing of a thirty-year defense treaty and other agreements with the Soviet Union in early 1950. However, in less than a decade Chinese internal developments were contributing to the demise of the lean-to-one-side policy. The Soviet Union, which had been providing economic aid and technical assistance on a large scale to the PRC since 1950, developed serious misgivings on both theoretical and practical grounds about China's grandiose program for instant GNP expansion known as the Great Leap Forward. When Peking challenged Soviet criticisms and ignored the advice of Soviet technicians, Moscow abruptly withdrew its aid personnel, dealing a servere blow to China's economy and triggering a drastic deterioration in Sino-Soviet economic ties.

The PRC's relations with the Soviet Union reached their lowest and most dangerous ebb during yet another interval of revolutionary ideology, the period of the Cultural Revolution. But the adverse international impact of the Cultural Revolution was by no means confined to the PRC's relations with the Soviet Union. The ideological frenzy exhibited by the Red Guards damaged the PRC's prestige around the world and alienated many hitherto staunch foreign admirers of "New China." At the height of the radical ascendancy in Peking, Albania seemed to be the only country the PRC regarded as friendly. All but one of the PRC's ambassadors abroad were recalled to Peking and its conventional diplomacy came to a virtual standstill. Foreign diplomats in Peking were harassed and the British Embassy was burned.

The ideological fervor of the Cultural Revolution also had violent repercussions in Hong Kong and Burma. In the case of the latter this violence resulted in the suspension of Chinese economic aid and a near break in diplomatic relations. Even the PRC's Communist neighbors, North Korea and North Vietnam, did not share the enthusiasm of the Red Guards for the export of Maoism, and their relations with the PRC cooled.

Thanks to an almost complete reversal of the "diplomacy" of the Cultural Revolution, China's foreign relations suffered no permanent damage from that great internal upheaval. But it serves as a dramatic recent example of the impact China's internal affairs can have on its foreign relations. Whether or not political contention in China again reaches the intensity of the Cultural Revolution, the direction taken by domestic policy will inevitably affect the PRC's relations with the rest of the world, and with its neighbors in particular. A brief examination of Chinese leadership factions, and the principal issues dividing them, is therefore pertinent to an analysis of the prospective course of Sino–Southeast Asian relations.

The Cultural Revolution revealed serious conflicts within the PRC's leadership, which theretofore had appeared to be remarkably cohesive. At its onset, the Chinese leadership fell into four principal groups: (1) Mao and his close associates, such as his wife, Chiang Ching, and his secretary, Chen Pota, and a group of Party radicals based in Shanghai and headed by Chang Chun-chiao; (2) the party bureaucracy, led by Head of State Liu Shao-chi and Secretary General Teng Hsiao-ping; (3) the government bureaucracy, headed by Premier Chou En-lai; and (4) the PLA, divided on strategy, but increasingly dominated by Defense Minister Lin Piao.[14]

The Cultural Revolution represented both a struggle for power and an attempt to change basic national policy. For some years before the Cultural Revolution, Mao had felt that he had been put on the political shelf by the Liu-Teng faction. Worse still, from Mao's point of view, the Party, under the direction of this faction, was taking China down the road of "revisionism" just as Khrushchev had taken the Soviet Union.[15] In order to regain control of the Party and put China back on a revolutionary course, Mao launched the Cultural Revolution with the support of his personal entourage and the Party radicals.

Liu and Teng were purged, along with a host of other Party bureaucrats. Many key officials of the government administrative hierarchy, which overlapped extensively with that of the Party, were also purged, leaving a political and administrative vacuum in China. Called in to quell the widespread disorders engendered by factional fighting, the PLA stayed on to run the country in the name of Mao. In the provinces it dominated the newly formed Revolutionary Committees and the reconstituted Party Committees.[16] At the Ninth Party Congress (held in Peking in April 1969) the PLA greatly enhanced its position in the central Party organs as well. Moreover, Defense Minister Lin Piao was formally designated as Mao's heir-apparent by the new Party constitution, an unprecedented step.

The eclipse of the civilian bureaucrats by the military did not last long, however. In the wake of Lin Piao's death in a plane crash in September 1971 and his subsequent disgrace as a plotter against Mao's life, the PLA's political fortunes waned. At the Tenth Party Congress in August 1973 the proportion of active military men elected to the Central Committee decreased from about half to less than one-third.[17] Perhaps even more significant was the transfer at the end of the year of eight of the eleven military regional commanders to other regional commands, seriously undermining their potent political bases in the provinces.[18]

The four-way division of the leadership at the onset of the Cultural Revolution had now become a three-way split, with the Party and government factions combining into one (sometimes called the Peking group), while the other two factions, the Party radicals (sometimes identified as the Shanghai group) and the PLA, retained essentially the same makeup. The Shanghai group, as before, was closest to Mao in outlook. It seemed to have unique access to the media and to exercise strong influence in the educational field. With Mao's apparent blessing this faction launched a series of polemical campaigns against the resurgent Party and government bureaucrats of the Peking group.

The first of these campaigns, ostensibly to criticize Lin Piao and Confucius, was launched in February 1974 with the announced purpose of saving China from falling back into revisionism.[19] It did not prove to be very effective. In fact, by disrupting production it may have done more to strengthen the hand of the moderate Peking group, which was emphasizing unity and stability, than to weaken it. In any case, it did not prevent the convening of the Fourth National People's Congress in January 1975, which in effect endorsed the "revisionist" economic priorities of the moderate faction.

Thus Premier Chou En-lai's "Report on the Work of the Government," which was approved by the Congress, held up "the comprehensive modernization of agriculture, industry, national defense, and science and technology before the end of the century" as China's "splendid goal."[20] The new constitution, also approved by the Congress, in Articles 5 and 7 endorsed material incentives in the form of sideline production and private plots, while Article 9 affirmed that the state should apply the principle: "From each according to his ability, to each according to his work."

The Fourth National People's Congress (NPC) also confirmed the return of many of the old "powerholders," purged during the Cultural Revolution, to government office. They were led by Teng Hsiao-ping, whose rise since his rehabilitation in 1973 had been spectacular. The PLA's loss of political influence was emphasized by Teng's appointment as PLA chief of staff, the first civilian ever to hold this position.[21] The radical faction's power within the Party was not reflected in the Fourth NPC's appointments to high government office, except for Chang Chun-chiao, who became head of the PLA's General Political Department as well as a deputy premier just behind Teng in rank. But it was not clear whether Chang's high offices reflected his abandonment of the radical faction or an effort to bring that group into a unified national leadership. Mao's conspicuous absence from the Fourth NPC also raised doubts about the extent to which unity had been achieved.

Within a month the radicals were displaying concern about the results of the Fourth NPC in a new polemical campaign keyed to Mao's directive to study the theory of the dictatorship of the proletariat. An editorial in the *People's Daily* warned that "new bourgeois elements may emerge from among a section of party members, workers, intellectuals and small producers."[22] This theme was elaborated by Yao Wen-yuan, a leading leftist writer and Politburo member credited with firing the first literary salvo of the Cultural Revolution. In an article in the theoretical journal,

Red Flag, Yao also warned of the emergence within the Party
of representatives of the bourgeoisie, and asserted that "the
bourgeois right . . . should be restricted under the dictatorship of the proletariat so that in the long course of socialist
revolution the three major differences between workers and
peasants, between town and country, and between mental
and manual labor will gradually be narrowed."[23]

Yao was clearly concerned that, unless they were brought
under control, the resurgent bureaucrat faction and its
policies would endanger the achievements of the Cultural
Revolution. Narrowing "the three major differences" is the
epitome of Maoist revolutionary values,[24] and was one of the
principal objectives of Cultural Revolution reforms.

In early September 1975 the radicals launched another
campaign aimed at preventing further backsliding from
Cultural Revolution achievements. Chairman Mao directed
that the classical novel, *The Water Margin*, be studied as a
negative example of "capitulationism" by high officials.
Although at the time the objective of this campaign was not
entirely clear,[25] it was subsequently linked with the criticism
of Lin Piao and Confucius and with the campaign to study
the dictatorship of the proletariat, in an important editorial
appearing in the three major Chinese publications on New
Year's Day 1976.[26]

This editorial, which accompanied two poems by Mao
first published in 1965, once again invoked Mao's support of
the radical attack on the "revisionist" policies of the moderate faction. Among other things, it attacked moderate criticism of higher education as "representing a Right deviation-
ist wind to reverse previous verdicts, [which] is a
conspicuous manifestation of the revisionist line that stands
against the proletariat on behalf of the bourgeoisie." Taking
as its special text Mao's dictum that "class struggle is the key
link and everything else hinges on it," the editorial declared

that "this has been Chairman Mao's fundamental theory and practice in leading our Party in carrying out socialist revolution over the past twenty years and more."

Hardly a week after this New Year's reaffirmation of Mao's priorities, Premier Chou En-lai died. Undoubtedly anticipating Chou's early death, the radicals were able to muster sufficient political strength (presumably including Mao's support) to block the widely anticipated appointment of Teng Hsiao-ping as Chou's successor. Instead, the relatively unknown Hua Kuo-feng was designated as acting premier, and a new campaign was launched against the moderates,

The significance of these leadership struggles lies not so much in who will govern in Peking as in how the issues that have divided the leadership will be resolved. One area where the opposing factions have come most sharply into conflict is that of education. It is here that the Cultural Revolution made perhaps its most significant impact.

Universities were closed from 1966 to 1970 and by 1975 had still not regained their pre–Cultural Revolution enrollments. More important still were the changes in their entrance requirements and curriculums when they did reopen. All high school graduates were required to work at least two years before they were eligible for consideration for university entrance. Those who gained admission were chosen more for their correct political thinking than for their academic attainments. University curriculums were drastically revised and shortened. On the other hand, the Cultural Revolution resulted in the opening of thousands of new schools in the countryside, making more education available to the peasants. In short, the PRC's education system since the Cultural Revolution has been turning out fewer and less well trained scientists, engineers, and others at the professional level, while giving more people more training at less sophisticated levels. It has thus made significant contributions toward the Maoist goal of reducing "the three major differences."

But the moderate faction has been dissatisfied with the quality of higher education produced by the Cultural Revolution reforms. For example, according to posters put up at the University of Peking in December 1975, the minister of education, Chou Yang, complained that "today's universities are training second-class workers" who are "not as good as high school students in the past politically or vocationally."[28] Another dissatisfied official was Liu Ping, deputy head of Tsinghua University, one of China's leading scientific institutions. He is reported to have warned in a letter to Mao that unless something were done to change the present educational system "people will be leaving universities without being able to read a book."[29]

The moderates' feelings about the state of scientific research in China have been summed up as follows: "Our science and technology are facing danger. These few years we blindly believed in self-sufficiency. Science is stagnating. Scientific research is backward. Too much preoccupation with politics and ideology hinders and damages scientific research."[30]

Despite a certain amount of hyperbole in these reported criticisms of the quality of higher education and research in China today, they do raise serious questions as to how far and how fast China can pursue the goals of modernization held up by Premier Chou En-lai at the Fourth National People's Congress. Foreign visitors have already noted the effect of the new educational system on the prospects for scientific research in China. Thus, in the fall of 1974, a group of American agricultural researchers visiting China was much impressed by the PRC's agricultural achievements, but they felt nevertheless that the disarray they found in agricultural research and training programs presented a long-run problem. They noted that few scientists had been trained in recent years and that nearly all the highly trained scientists they had encountered were over 60 years of age.[31]

The Cultural Revolution's educational system not only impairs the growth of China's own scientific and technological capabilities, but it also limits the PRC's ability to absorb foreign technology. According to a recent American study, the educational emphasis in China since the Cultural Revolution "could not help but retard the devleopment of a technical labor force with skill and educational standards comparable to those of the Western World. It takes decades to develop such a force," this study points out, "and a present deficiency could well act as a serious brake on China's rate of technological modernization."[32] Those in China who attach importance to rapid economic growth and modernization have come to the same conclusion, judging by the attacks on the present educational system by responsible officials such as Chou Yang and Liu Ping.

The question of absorption of foreign technology points up another conflict between the two lines—again a conflict of emphasis and priority rather than of absolute opposites. Both the moderates and the radicals subscribe to the general principle of self-reliance in China's economic development. But for the sake of accelerating economic growth and modernization the moderates are willing to compromise the principle to a greater extent than the radicals. Thus, during the Cultural Revolution, when radical politics commanded China's policies, acquisition of foreign technology was sharply curtailed, and by 1969 machinery imports had dropped to one-fourth of previous peak levels.[33] After the Cultural Revolution, however, and especially since 1973, the PRC began purchasing large numbers of complete plants. These plant acquisitions have affected a few areas basic to China's economic growth and the feeding and clothing of its people.[34]

A good example of the importance of these acquisitions is furnished by China's purchase of thirteen giant chemical fertilizer plants in 1973-74. As one American expert has put it: "Until production from these plants becomes available, Chinese agricultural development will be more or less a holding action."[35] This is because a significant increase in the rate of growth of agriculture depends, among other things, on substantial increases in the availability of chemical fertilizer. Thus, although only 6 to 8 percent of China's annual technology increase is achieved through imports,[36] these imports are indispensable to the attainment of the kind of economic growth goals put forward by Chou En-lai and approved by the Fourth National People's Congress.

However, large-scale purchases of fertilizer and other ultramodern high-technology equipment, which have characterized Chinese policy since the resurgence of the moderate faction, undermine Mao's revolutionary priorities. They increase China's dependence on foreign trade and thus its exposure to capitalist contamination. Moreover, such purchases have created deficits in China's balance of payments which may force Peking to resort to foreign borrowing, a practice it has assiduously avoided on ideological grounds. While the PRC's rapidly growing oil exports may well rescue it from serious balance-of-payments trouble, even those oil exports will in a sense tie the Chinese economy more closely to the economies of the industrialized countries, especially to Japan's. Importation of sophisticated foreign technology, furthermore, creates a demand for more highly trained technical and professional personnel, thus emphasizing the need for improving the quality of higher education, with the consequent risk of widening "the three differences."

Another important area of conflict obviously involves the PLA, which itself has been divided on what China's defense strategy should be and on its priorities in the development of weapons systems. Differences on national defense policy resulted in the first notable purge of the Cultural Revolution, that of Lo Jui-ching, PLA chief of staff.

Lo differed from the Maoists on strategy in at least three respects: he placed more reliance on regular forces than on local forces or the militia; he tempered the Maoist strategy of "luring deep" with calls for the establishment of prepared defense positions fairly close to portions of the Chinese border; and he advocated rapid improvement in China's air defense.[37] Typical of the conflict of the two lines, Lo's strategy called for more emphasis on technical training and technically advanced weaponry than that of the Maoists, who emphasized the importance of the PLA's political training above all.

The issue of national defense strategy is, of course, extremely complex. To reduce it merely to a question of the priorities of technical vs. political training, of sophisticated weaponry vs. guerrilla tactics, would be to oversimplify it. The resurgence of the moderate faction after the Cultural Revolution did not bring a general expansion of high-technology weapons systems, which would inevitably have meant an expanded military budget. On the contrary, there was an apparent reduction in military expenditures between 1971 and 1975. Some of the possible reasons for this reduction have little to do with the conflict between the two lines—for example, the decline in military expenditures more or less coincided with the demise of Lin Piao and the consequent decline in the PLA's political influence. It may also have resulted from a Chinese perception of a decreased American threat, or from Peking's feeling that its nuclear and conventional forces are sufficiently strong to deter a Soviet attack, or from inadequacies in the PRC's military research and development effort.[38] But the overriding cause was probably Peking's decision to give priority to economic growth, especially in the agricultural sector.

Such an assessment is consistent with statements made by the Chinese leadership, such as that by Deputy Premier Teng Hsiao-ping to a delegation of American university presidents visiting China in the fall of 1974. Explaining that China could not afford to compete with the Soviet Union in advanced weaponry, Teng is quoted as saying: "if we made these bombs, we could not have enough food to feed ourselves nor clothes to clothe ourselves." He went on to stress the importance of agriculture by pointing out that it not only feeds the population and supplies raw materials to light industry but also gradually provides capital for investment in heavy industry.[39]

Teng's remarks did not mean that the PRC has given up making nuclear weapons, missiles, and other sophisticated equipment. Peking is continuing to modernize its armed forces, and its naval building program has been especially significant in recent years. Moreover, costs will inevitably go up, causing Chinese military leaders to demand larger resource allocations for the defense establishment.[40] Such PLA demands will impinge on the priorities of the other two major political power centers. If they mean substantially increasing the percentage of China's GNP devoted to defense, they jeopardize the economic development priorities of the moderate faction. If they create requirements for new, high-technology equipment, either domestic or foreign, they endanger the Maoist policy of reducing "the three major differences."

A problem which has troubled all three leadership groups, but for different reasons, is that of urban workers' discontent, or "bourgeois factionalism," as it has been labelled in the Chinese media.[41] Such discontent led to serious labor unrest in parts of China in 1974-75, requiring prolonged intervention by the PLA in some cases. Workers' demands for better material rewards for their labors appeared to be at the heart of the unrest, although it may have sprung from other causes as well. This "bourgeois factionalism," probably so labelled by the radicals, offends the latter by its demands for greater material incentives, which would widen the differences between worker and peasant and between town and country. By disrupting production and defying authority it sins in the eyes of the moderate faction and the PLA. The former may also feel that the workers' wage claims compete unacceptably with agricultural development for funds.

Thus fundamental policy issues divide the leadership in the PRC, as in other countries. But in the PRC these divisions have been complicated and exacerbated by the long, indecisive ideological conflict between the two lines— between "socialist construction" and "revisionism." For a time after Chou En-lai's death Mao's dictum that "class struggle" takes precedence over unity and stability, over economic growth and modernization, seemed to be gaining the ascendancy. It seemed possible that the radical faction would be able to slow down, if not stem, the tide of "reversing" the verdicts of the Cultural Revolution that had been flowing since the resurgence of the moderates. But the swift repression of the champions of Mao's revolutionary priorities so soon after his death seems now to ensure that this tide will continue to flow. The same three publications which on January 1, 1976, reaffirmed the priority of "class struggle" pledged on October 25 that Chou En-lai's economic growth and modernization priorities would be implemented.[42] Once again the economic imperatives underlying the policies of the moderate faction—policies which were restored after the Maoist paroxysms of the Great Leap Forward and the Great Proletarian Cultural Revolution—seem to have prevailed. Such policies give the PRC a stake in a stable world and regional order, and in reasonably free international economic intercourse, a stake shared by China's Southeast Asian neighbors.

2

Peking-Oriented Insurgencies

While the events in China following Mao's death indicate that the pragmatic Chinese domestic and foreign policies of the last half-dozen years or so are likely to continue, this does not mean that Peking will turn its back on Communist revolutionary movements in Southeast Asia. Peking's emphasis on state relations in recent years has not meant that it has abandoned its support of "just struggles" of oppressed peoples, a point that Chou En-lai himself took pains to make. On the other hand, it is a Maoist belief that only the people of the country can carry out a successful revolution in that country, a belief that ensures the nonintervention of Chinese military personnel except in cases where Peking perceives China's national security to be involved.

The concept of revolutionary self-reliance, however, does not inhibit, though it may limit, other forms of Chinese

assistance, such as political and military training, propaganda support, and provision of arms. Communist movements in Southeast Asia have in the past received these types
of support from the PRC. In terms of its own rationale,
Peking has a wide range of choice as to the amount and kind
of assistance it may furnish Peking-oriented insurgents in
Southeast Asia, while never needing to shoulder the burden
of responsibility for their victories or defeats.[43]

Peking's support of armed revolutionary movements is
resented and feared by the non-Communist governments of
the region. It has been a major factor in delaying the
normalization of state relations between some of these
governments and Peking. As Indonesian Foreign Minister
Adam Malik once succinctly put it: "In my opinion China
will be more popular in Southeast Asia if they stop subver-
sion. It is in China's own interest as well as in the interest of
the countries of the region."[44]

Indeed, when Malaysia entered into diplomatic relations
with the PRC in 1974 its prime minister is reported to have
sought and received assurances that Peking would do just
that. Unhappily, Malaysia's establishment of state relations
with the PRC did not bring a cessation either of Communist
insurgency or of Peking's encouragement of it. This should
not have been surprising to the Malaysian government,
which had had ample opportunity to study Burma's twenty-
five years of maintaining diplomatic relations with the PRC,
while it combated Peking-supported insurgency.

Peking does not hide its two-track approach to foreign
relations, but proclaims it even at the moment when diplomatic relations are being established. Thus Premier Chou
En-lai asserted on May 31, 1974, at a welcoming banquet in
Peking for Prime Minister Razak of Malaysia: "The Chinese
people consistently support the just struggles of all oppressed peoples. This is our internationalist duty. We hold at

the same time that a social system of a country can only be chosen and decided by its own people and cannot be imposed by other countries. Countries with different social systems can develop state relations on the basis of the five principles."[45] Much the same thing was said by Vice Premier Teng Hsiao-ping at welcoming banquets in Peking a year later for President Marcos of the Philippines and Prime Minister Kukrit Pramoj of Thailand.[46]

Peking's practice of supporting "just struggles" in Southeast Asia while it simultaneously conducts "state relations" with the government being struggled against has caused the PRC to be accused of having two policies—party policy and government policy.[47] This may be true to a limited extent, reflecting failures of coordination within the far-flung Chinese bureaucracy, parts of which are charged with conducting state relations while other parts deal with foreign Communist parties. But in the last analysis there is only one policy—that of the Communist Party of China (CPC).

The supremacy of the Party is spelled out anew in the "Constitution of the People's Republic of China" adopted by the Fourth National People's Congress on January 17, 1975. According to Article 2 of the constitution, "The Communist Party of China is the core leadership of the whole Chinese people." Article 16 says, "The National People's Congress is the highest organ of state power under the leadership of the Communist Party of China." The prime minister and other ministers of the government are appointed "on the proposal of the Central Committee of the Communist Party of China."[48]

Rather than representing party policy and government policy, Peking's support of insurgency and its maintenance of state relations represent two strands of one policy—the PRC's ideological aspirations, on the one hand, and its

pragmatic, national interests on the other. While in some
periods since its founding in 1949 the PRC has emphasized
ideological considerations over pragmatic interests, both the
ideological and pragmatic strands have consistently been
present in its foreign policy. Shifts in the PRC's domestic
priorities (as indicated in the previous chapter) and changing perceptions of opportunities and dangers abroad have
determined which strand will be emphasized.[49]

Thus, despite Peking's present emphasis on state relations, Chinese support of insurgencies in Southeast Asia will
continue. A brief look at the current state of these insurgencies may shed some light on the extent and nature of such
support and on its effect on Sino–Southeast Asian relations.

The Communist triumph in Indochina in the spring of
1975 can hardly have failed to hearten proponents of armed
revolution in Southeast Asia, while arousing apprehension
on the part of non-Communist Southeast Asian governments. The latter's fears have centered particularly on North
Vietnam and how it will dispose of the vast supply of
American arms captured in South Vietnam. Such worries
were expressed, for example, by Prime Minister Lee Kwan
Yew of Singapore in a speech to The Asia Society in New
York on May 12, 1975, as follows: "The negative factors are
incipient rebellious groups who may now come into possession of part of the vast armoury of weapons which the
Communists captured in South Vietnam and Cambodia. If
these weapons go into a 'swords into ploughshares' pro-
gramme then peace and stability is almost guaranteed for
Southeast Asia. However, it is doubtful if the new owners of
these American-made weapons have these priorities, now
that they have won their 'war of national liberation.'"[50]

The country most immediately threatened by the repercussions of the Communist victory in Indochina is Thailand.
Not only does it have common borders with Laos and

Cambodia, but Communist insurgents in northeast Thailand have long been receiving logistical support from the Pathet Lao and the North Vietnamese across these borders.[51] Thai insurgents have been trained in North Vietnam since the early 1960s. A camp at Hoa Binh is reported to have graduated sixty-two Thai recruits as early as 1962.[52] In the fall of 1975 Thai Prime Minister Kukrit Pramoj, in answer to a press question, flatly asserted that he had evidence of Hanoi's support of insurgent movements in Thailand. Said Kukrit: "We have captured arms; we have captured insurgents; we have talked to them and we know by our intelligence that the insurgents were trained in North Vietnam."[53]

While the Thai insurgents have received military training in North Vietnam, their political leadership cadres were generally trained in China. Moreover, since 1962 the principal propaganda organ of the Communist Party of Thailand (CPT) has operated from Chinese soil. Typical of the line taken by this radio transmitting station was a broadcast on December 1, 1974, marking the thirty-second anniversary of the founding of the CPT, which called for "seizing power by armed force" and establishing "the people's government."[54]

In addition to the northeast, Communist insurgent bases are located in northern Thailand and in the southern isthmus, while over 1,800 Malaysian-oriented Communist terrorists also operate in southern Thailand's borderlands.[55] In the country as a whole the number of insurgents has grown from an estimated 1,200 in 1965 to as many as 10,000 in 1975.[56] The failure of Thai governments to halt the growth of insurgency in recent years appears to stem from some of the same weaknesses that contributed to the downfall of neighboring Indo-Chinese governments. The gap between the cities (especially Bangkok) and the villages has grown dangerously. Civilian officials have been indifferent to rural problems or unable to deal with them effectively.

Similarly, the military have been reluctant to take the offensive and loath to stray far from their camps.[57]

But it would be premature to write Thailand off as the next victim of armed Communist revolution. Despite their growth in recent years, the insurgents are still relatively few in number, and they too have fundamental weaknesses. The greatest of these is one shared by their counterparts elsewhere in Southeast Asia: an inability to identify their cause with nationalism, by far the strongest political force in the region. They have no nationally known leader such as Ho Chi Minh, and no national symbol remotely corresponding to the king of Thailand.

Moreover, the insurgents in Thailand do not have the kind of targets which were so helpful in putting nationalism into the service of the Communists in Vietnam—colonialism, reunification of the fatherland, and foreign intervention. Independent Thailand has never been a colony, nor is it partitioned. While the American military presence in Thailand has furnished a foreign-intervention target, it is hardly comparable to that presented in Vietnam, and in any case it is a greatly diminished one.

The insurgents in Thailand do exploit nationalism of a sort, that of the ethnic minorities such as the Meo in the north, the Lao in the northeast, and the Malays in the south. These minorities have furnished much of the insurgents' fighting force, and the insurgents' principal bases are located in areas mainly inhabited by minority peoples. But the exploitation of minority animosities against the Bangkok government cuts two ways. To the extent that it identifies the insurgents' cause with minority nationalism it alienates the Thais who make up about 85 percent of the country's population. Added to this is the handicap the insurgents suffer from being identified with their foreign supporters, the Chinese and North Vietnamese. Direct intervention by

North Vietnamese troops would of course allow the Thai government to rally Thai nationalism even more effectively in its favor.

But direct intervention of North Vietnamese troops, which was so important to ultimate Communist victory in Indochina, seems unlikely in Thailand. The overriding mission of the North Vietnamese in Indochina was the "liberation" of South Vietnam. They found it necessary to use the territory of Laos and Cambodia for this purpose, and they did. But they have no remotely comparable reason to intervene in Thai territory. Moverover, although the North Vietnamese have been providing aid to the Thai insurgents in the northeast, they are not bound to them by the kind of ties that cemented their relations with the Cambodian and Lao Communist parties, which sprang originally from one Indo-Chinese movement dominated by the Vietnamese. As already noted, the historical links of the CPT have been with China. In short, Hanoi does not have the kind of motivation to intervene in Thailand that it had in neighboring Indo-Chinese states.

A further restraint on military intervention by Hanoi is Thailand's international position. In the traditional Thai manner, Bangkok scrambled quickly to adjust to Communist victory and the defeat of U.S. policies in Indochina, an adjustment made easier by the fact that it was already under way well before the final demise of the Thieu and Lon Nol governments. For at least two years the Thai government had been moving in the direction of establishing diplomatic relations with Peking, abolishing barriers to trade with China, and in other ways making clear its desire for normalization of Sino-Thai relations. At the same time Thailand began loosening its links with the United States, especially its military ties, a process merely accelerated rather than inaugurated by the Communist triumph in Indochina.

These adjustments were climaxed on August 6, 1976, a little more than a month after the formal reunification of Vietnam, with the establishment of diplomatic relations between Bangkok and Hanoi.

Further reducing any incentive Hanoi might have to intervene in Thailand is Bangkok's membership in the Association of Southeast Asian Nations (ASEAN). Hanoi cannot afford to risk hostilities with this important regional group, whose idea of making Southeast Asia a neutral zone has received Peking's endorsement.[58]

In sum, neither domestic nor international conditions are as favorable for Communist armed revolution in Thailand as they were in Indochina. The prospects of the Thai Communist insurgents seizing national power are at best long range. But such prospects exist and could conceivably be realized unless Thailand can effectively come to grips with its social and economic problems, especially those of the countryside.

The insurgency situation in Burma, though generally worse than that in Thailand, is less subject to the influence of the Communist victory in Indochina. This is due in part to the fact that Burma is less geographically exposed to Indochina than is Thailand, but principally to the BCP's long-standing ties with Peking. There is no evidence that North Vietnam has played a role in the BCP insurgency.

Perhaps because of Burma's strategic importance to China, Peking has attached particular significance to Communist insurgency in Burma. As early as 1949 the Chinese Communist Party rated the revolution in Burma just behind that in Vietnam in importance.[59] The amount of support Peking has provided the BCP since then has varied, affected in good part by China's internal developments. Thus at the height of Liu Shao-chi's influence in the early 1960s Sino-Burmese state relations flourished, to the detriment of the

BCP. But when the Cultural Revolution swept Liu and the "moderates" from power in China, Liu's policies toward Burma were denounced by the Red Guards and Sino-Burmese state relations nearly foundered, while Chinese support of the BCP reached unprecedented levels.

The period of the Cultural Revolution brought important changes to the BCP. Its leadership was torn by ideological dissension and rent by purges, climaxed in 1968 by the assassination of its prestigious chairman, Thankin Than Tun. He was replaced by Takin Zin, while Thakin Ba Thein Tin, long a resident of Peking, became the new vice chairman. More importantly, the BCP's principal military base was shifted from the Pegu Yomas in central Burma to the China border area, where a "northeast command" was set up under Naw Seng, a former Kachin sergeant in the Burmese army who had defected to the BCP around 1950 and had then been sent to China for training. The northeast command's forces were largely recruited from the hill peoples of the border area and trained and equipped in China. These BCP forces (as previously noted) overran thousands of square miles of Burmese territory adjacent to the Chinese borders between 1971 and 1973.

Meanwhile, the remaining BCP insurgents in the Pegu Yomas from time to time have raided government communications lines in central Burma and have been attacked in turn by the Burmese army. On March 21, 1975, the Burmese government announced that its army had captured BCP headquarters in the Pegu Yomas and found the bodies of BCP Chairman Thakin Zin and Secretary Thakin Chit. According to a government spokesman, the "main trunk of communism" in Burma had been felled.[60]

In announcing this victory, the Burmese government, typically, stressed that the BCP insurgents were backed by a "foreign power" while pointing out that the government

had achieved this success without foreign aid in either
weapons or personnel. With themes of this sort, the Burmese
government has consistently played on Burman nationalism
to undermine the appeal not only of the BCP insurgents but
also of the non-Communist rebel groups which have operated in the Thailand-Burma border areas with varying degrees
of support from Thailand. The failure of the BCP and other
insurgents to make significant progress in areas inhabited
mainly by the majority Burman race must be attributed in
great measure to their inability to identify their cause with
Burmese nationalism. At the same time their attempts to pin
the label of "imperialist running dog" on the Rangoon
government have been largely nullified by Burma's long-
standing adherence to a policy of strict nonalignment in its
foreign relations, and by its go-it-alone socialist posture
domestically.

On the other hand, the Burmese government has enjoyed
little success in its efforts to eliminate insurgency in areas
inhabited mainly by the non-Burman ethnic minorities,
which collectively account for over 25 percent of the country's population. In these areas local nationalism works
against the national government (almost exclusively Burman in composition) and is utilized by the BCP to recruit
antigovernment forces. However, the BCP has been unable
to penetrate some of the more important ethnic insurgent
groups, such as the Kachin Independence Army. The pa-
rochialism of the hill tribesmen which hinders Rangoon's
efforts to promote national unity also handicaps the Communists.[61]

While the Burmese government's claim that the BCP
strongholds in the Irrawaddy Delta and in central Burma
have been destroyed may be substantially correct, its claim to
have felled the "main trunk of Communism" seems exagger-
ated. The BCP still controls vast tracts of hill country in

eastern Burma for which China provides the "secure rear" so important to Mao Tse-tung's guerrilla strategy. From this rear area the PRC can be expected to continue to provide training, arms, and advisers for the BCP's forces under the leadership of Thakin Ba Thein Tin, who is Peking's man. In fact, the Central Committee of the CPC has already assured the BCP and its leaders of its confidence that they will "win thorough and complete victory in their revolutionary war."[62]

Malaysia has the distinction of harboring two separate Peking-oriented Communist insurgencies: that of the Communist Party of Malaysia (CPM) in West Malaysia and that of the North Kalimantan Communist Party (NKCP) in East Malaysia. Both of these rebellions have depended heavily on support from the ethnic Chinese minority of Malaysia, which constitutes about 34 percent of its population.

The CPM emerged from World War II with valuable experience in guerrilla fighting against the Japanese, which also made its leaders popular heroes in the Chinese community. When the CPM turned its talents to fighting the British for Malaya's freedom, it had a strong appeal for all races in the country. But after the British granted independence to Malaya in 1957, the CPM "terrorists" were no longer able to enlist Malayan nationalism in their cause and they "soon dwindled down to a hard core hiding out on the Thailand frontier of Malaya."[63]

Though somewhat more tardily than other Southeast Asian Communist insurgents, the CPM responded to the militant calls for revolution emanating from Peking during the Cultural Revolution period and by mid-1968 had begun to revive its terrorist activites. Its attacks were directed not only against the Malaysian authorities but also against the Thai. Moreover, it began to coordinate its activities for the first time with those of the Thai insurgents who had infiltrated into southern Thailand. In 1969 a powerful China-based radio facility calling itself Voice of the People of Malaya began broadcasting exhortations to the CPM to carry on the armed struggle.

The cultural and communications gap between the largely Malay and Moslem rural population of West Malaysia and the largely Chinese, non-Moslem "terrorists" handicapped the CPM in its efforts to use the villages to surround the cities and seize political power by armed force—to repeat the familiar litany of the Maoists.[64] On the other hand, a kind of ethnic nationalism felt by Chinese in Malaysia has undoubtedly played an important part in the persistence of the Peking-oriented CPM insurgency. After the serious race-rioting between Chinese and Malays in May 1969, the CPM condemned "Malay chauvinism" and "special Malay rights" in a rather obvious appeal to this Chinese nationalism.[65]

The Malaysian government hoped that its establishment of diplomatic relations with the PRC would undermine the CPM's ethnocentric appeal to Malaysians of Chinese origin. It would demonstrate that China supported the Malaysian government rather than the CPM. Thus, upon his return from Peking to Kuala Lumpur in June 1974, Prime Minister Razak asserted that he had received "categorical assurances" from Chairman Mao and Premier Chou that China considered the insurgency in Malaysia a "purely internal problem to be dealt with as we see fit."[66] Whatever the assurances may have been that Razak brought back from Peking, they did not bring a halt to the CPM's armed rebellion. In fact there has been an upsurge in terrorist incidents since 1974. This has caused the Malaysian government to revive many of the measures of the emergency period of the 1950s. Thus it has reintroduced measures to control population movements and other legal provisions of that period. Households must

report all movements of members and guests. A compulsory vigilante organization has been set up to conduct patrols, and special courts have been revived to obtain speedy convictions of the CPM terrorists and their supporters.[67]

Premier Razak is reported to have sought further assurance from the Chinese ambassador in May 1975 that the PRC would not "export revolution."[68] Razak's action was apparently triggered by a message from the Central Committee of the CPC to the Central Committee of the CPM, dated April 29, 1975, extending "warm fraternal congratulations" on the forty-fifth anniversary of the CPM's founding. After complimenting the CPM on its progress, the CPC declared: "We firmly believe that the revolutionary armed struggle of the Malayan people will certainly triumph."[69] While such messages from Peking can be shrugged off as the ritualistic rhetoric of revolutionary ideologues, when they are translated into ambushes and assassinations, as they have continued to be in Malaysia since its establishment of diplomatic relations with the PRC, they quite naturally undermine Malaysian confidence in such ties.

In East Malaysia (North Kalimantan) there has been no upsurge of terrorist activity similar to that occurring in West Malaysia since 1974. The heyday of the Communist insurgency there was achieved during the period of Indonesia's "confrontation" of the newly-formed state of Malaysia in the early 1960s. The Indonesian army and the Indonesian Communists (who were then collaborating with President Sukarno) trained and armed about 800 Sarawak Communist guerrillas.[70] But with the settlement between Indonesia and Malaysia of June 1966, ending "confrontation," the Sarawak Communist insurgents found themselves hunted by the Indonesian as well as by the Malaysian army. They split into two groups. One group settled in a remote part of Indonesian Borneo along the Sarawak border. The other, larger

group took an active part with the Indonesian Communists
in launching terrorist attacks on the Indonesian army.

By January 1969, according to Indonesian claims, the
original band of several hundred East Malaysian insurgents
had been reduced to about 70.[71] The NKCP was further
weakened in March 1974 when one of its leaders, Bong Kee-
chok, surrendered to the government with 481 of his follow-
ers in response to a virtual amnesty. The following month,
the chairman of the NKCP Central Committee, Wen Ming-
chuan, issued a statement carried by the New China News
Agency (NCNA) denouncing Bong's surrender and declar-
ing that the NKCP would "continue to use armed struggle as
the main form of struggle."[72] However, the NKCP has not
been able to emulate the armed upsurge of its counterpart in
West Malaysia.

Singapore is the only Southeast Asian country which has
no national Communist Party. Members of its Communist
underground movement belong to the CPM. Unlike Communists in neighboring countries, those in Singapore have
not pursued the path of armed struggle "as the main form of
struggle," perhaps because Singapore is a city-state without
extensive hinterland where guerrilla operations can be
based.

Nevertheless, Singapore's Communists have resorted to
violence and terrorism on occasion. As recently as the
summer of 1975, the Singapore government announced that
four men and a woman had been detained "for their active
involvement in the activities of the Communist Party of
Malaya (CPM) in Singapore" and that two arms caches had
been seized. The government's announcement stated further:
"The arrests and the recovery of arms and ammunition and
communist books and literature go to show that far from
being dormant in Singapore, the CPM continues to clandes-
tinely rebuild its shattered organization. . . . It is also evident

that these CPM elements, despite the changed conditions in Singapore today, still persist in pursuing their objective of establishing a communist Malaya, including Singapore, through acts of violence."[73]

While the Communists in Singapore have by no means eschewed violence, their chosen political instrument has been the *Barisan Socialis* (Socialist Front), Singapore's principal opposition political party. However, the *Barisan Socialis* has been weakened by internal dissension, and in the 1972 elections it failed to win a single parliamentary seat.[74] Nevertheless, the existence of the *Barisan Socialis*, whch is even more Chinese-oriented than the CPM, gives a special political sensitivity to Singapore's relations with the PRC. Although the Singapore government itself is dominated by Chinese, who make up about 75 percent of the country's population, ideological affinity might tempt an official Peking establishment in Singapore, such as an embassy, to exploit the "Chineseness" of the *Barisan Socialis* against the government, posing difficult security problems.

In the Philippines, as elsewhere in Southeast Asia, Communist insurgency was given renewed impetus by the Cultural Revolution in China. For years the Philippine Communist Party (PKP) had been following a largely nonviolent united front strategy, but in 1967-68 it split into pro-Peking and pro-Moscow factions, with the former advocating agrarian revolution and armed struggle along Maoist lines.[75] This split followed a visit to China in May 1967 by the leader of the pro-Peking group within the PKP, José Maria Sison, and a Peking radio broadcast on May 23 of an alleged statement by the Politburo of the PKP supporting "true armed struggle" as the only path to national and social liberation, and committing the PKP "to an uncompromising struggle against modern revisionism with the Soviet revisionist ruling clique at its center." Subsequently the pro-Moscow

faction of the PKP Politburo issued its own statement
denouncing the pro-Peking faction's statement as "spur-
ious" and opposing its call to arms.[76] On December 28, 1968,
the pro-Peking faction, now calling itself the PKP(M/L)
opened a Congress of Re-establishment of the PKP, where it
drew up a program based on Mao Tse-tung's thought and
accepting Peking's international leadership. Consistent
with its dedication to armed struggle, the PKP(M/L) in
March 1969 formed the New People's Army (NPA) under a
former HUK leader, Commander Dante.[77]

Since its formation the NPA has pursued the armed
struggle against the Philippine government with mixed
success. Its principal stronghold has been Luzon, but its
activities have spread to other islands as well, including the
Visayan Islands and Mindanao. NPA operations expanded
in Mindanao during 1975 but were set back in the Visayans
and parts of Luzon; Filipino military sources reported that
in the provinces around Davao NPA forces "had been
making their presence heavily felt since June."[78] While there
is no apparent connection, it is somewhat ironic that intensified NPA activity in Mindanao should have occurred just
when the Philippines and the PRC were establishing diplomatic relations.

For its part, the pro-Moscow branch of the PKP made
peace with the Philippine government in the fall of 1974,
giving as its reasons the government's land reform program
and its new foreign policy of seeking to improve relations
with the socialist states and the Arab countries. Since elements of this wing of the PKP had been frequently subjected
to armed attack by the NPA, it is possible they made peace
with the government primarily for safety's sake.[79]

To what extent Peking has supported the PKP(M/L) and
the NPA outside of the propanganda field is not entirely
clear. In 1972 Premier Chou En-lai is reported to have

acknowledged to President Marcos' special envoy, Ambassador Romauldez, that "Lin Piao elements" had trained dissidents in the Philippines but this was no longer taking place.[80] Nevertheless, a shipwreck in the South China Sea some time after Chou gave these assurances revealed a shipment of Chinese arms bound for the Philippines, and the surviving members of the crew asked for asylum in China.[81]

How much assistance will be provided from the PRC to the NPA in the future will presumably depend on a variety of factors, such as the state of "state relations" between Peking and Manila, the viability of the NPA, and the relative influence of ideological and pragmatic considerations in Chinese policy. Even more than in the case of the Communist insurgencies in mainland Southeast Asian countries, the prospects for success of the NPA depend primarily on the effectiveness of its own efforts and on the ability of the national government to cope with the country's pressing economic and social problems rather than on outside assistance.

Aside from Singapore, Indonesia is the only non-Communist Southeast Asian country which does not have a significant Communist insurgency problem. Yet in none of the other countries have the Communists come as close as in Indonesia to the achievement of national power, which may explain why the Indonesian government has been the most cautious of the Southeast Asian governments about normalizing relations with the PRC. In the early 1960s, thanks to President Sukarno's policy of friendship with the PRC abroad and political alliance with the Indonesian Communist Party (PKI) at home, and to the PKI's decision to lean toward Peking in the context of the Sino-Soviet quarrel, Chinese influence in Indonesia reached levels unprecedented in any non-Communist country. The extent of Jakarta's collaboration with Peking is illustrated by the presence of seventeen delegations from Indonesia (including government, military, and PKI representatives) in the visitors' gallery at the Chinese national day celebrations on October 1, 1965, in Peking, and by the seven Sino-Indonesian agreements which had been signed the day before. These agreements "only added to the pile of agreements, protocols, and joint communiqués between the two governments that had been produced with increasing frequency over the previous 12 months."[82]

But at that very moment Peking's Indonesian idyll was being destroyed by an ill-advised and ill-timed coup attempt in Jakarta supported by the PKI. This attempted coup brought to power the very anti-Communist military leaders who had been targeted for liquidation, and resulted in the decimation of the PKI's own leadership. Only one of the ten members or candidate members of the PKI's Politburo escaped the vengeance of the Indonesian army.[83] In March 1966 the PKI was outlawed and in 1967 diplomatic relations with the PRC were suspended by the Indonesian government.

Since its fall from near-power following the abortive September 30 coup, the PKI has been further weakened by the split in its ranks caused by the Sino-Soviet quarrel. As in the case of the PKP, the split developed during the Cultural Revolution in China and reflected a clash between the Chinese emphasis on armed struggle and the more gradualist Soviet approach. In the summer of 1967, at the height of radical influence over Chinese foreign policy, Peking called for a general uprising throughout Indonesia. PKI elements responded with armed terrorism in East Java and (combined with Sarawakian Chinese Communists) in West Kalimantan, but the result was only to further undermine PKI strength.[84] Although in the summer of 1975 "several hundred rebels" were reported to be still "darting back and forth across the Sarawak border into West Kalimantan,"[85] the PKI insurgency in Indonesia as a whole has been negligible for some years.

Yet Peking's support of the PKI rebellion and its continuing succor of PKI leaders have blocked the resumption of Sino-Indonesian state relations. President Suharto put it plainly in a speech before the People's Consultative Congress (MRP) in early 1973: "With the People's Republic of China which manifestly supported the September 30 PKI rebellion, we are willing to resume diplomatic relations provided it really demonstrates a friendly attitude towards us, is not hostile to us, and ceases to render assistance and facilities to former PKI leaders who were positively involved in the rebellion."[86] In effect, Jakarta is saying to Peking that resumption of "state relations" with Indonesia must depend on the PRC's giving up support of "just struggles" against the Indonesian government. This Peking has not been willing to do, and Sino-Indonesian diplomatic relations are still "frozen."

Moreover, Peking is likely to continue its support of "just struggles" by PRC-oriented Communist parties. Though they may not like it, Indonesia and its neighbors will have to put up with it if they want to normalize state relations with the PRC. The trend among them to establish diplomatic relations with China indicates their acceptance of this reality. But Peking's continued support of Communist insurgencies, even when confined to the propaganda level, is bound to influence these relations adversely. Malaysian Prime Minister Razak's reaction to the CPC's message of April 25, 1975, congratulating the CPM on its forty-fifth anniversary, has already been noted. A "senior Malaysian official" is reported to have observed that Sino-Malaysian relations would have blossomed if that message had not been sent.[87]

The CPC's greeting to the PKI on May 22, 1975, provides another example of Peking's propaganda support of Southeast Asian Communist parties which has blighted state relations. In its message the CPC described the PKI as the "core leading the Indonesian people's revolution" and declared: "Our two Parties have always sympathized with and supported each other in the protracted revolutionary struggles."[88] President Suharto has reportedly indicated that in view of this message hopes for a swift rapprochement with China would have to be postponed.[89]

While it is difficult to measure the amount of clandestine material support Communist insurgents in Southeast Asia may have received from the PRC recently, on the basis of overt indications such support does not appear to have grown in the wake of the Communist triumph in Indochina. In fact, in Burma, where Chinese material support of insurgency has been far larger than in any other Southeast Asian country, the indications are that such support has fallen off. Significantly, for the first time in some years the BCP launched no dry-season offensive in 1975-76. Nevertheless, Southeast Asian governments will be skeptical of Peking's official assurances of noninterference as long as the CPC openly proclaims its support of fraternal Parties bent on overthrowing them.

3

Overseas Chinese

The presence of millions of Overseas Chinese in Southeast Asia, like the presence of Peking-oriented insurgencies, gives a special dimension to Sino-Southeast Asian relations. The highly organized, tightly knit Chinese immigrant communities have resisted assimilation. Their traditional loyalty to China has affronted the burgeoning nationalism of the region, and their commercial success has aroused local resentment despite the fact that they have contributed to the economic growth of their adopted countries.

Policies pursued by Chinese governments from the time of the Revolution of 1911 to the early 1950s contributed much to the political and cultural isolation of the Overseas Chinese communities. Chiefly responsible was China's treatment of all persons of Chinese race as Chinese citizens regardless of where they were born or of what other citizen-

ship they might acquire abroad. China's broad application
of the principle that the citizenship of the father is automatically conferred on his children meant that Chinese families
that had lived for generations in Southeast Asia were claimed
as citizens by the Chinese government and enjoyed its protection.

In the years when the Kuomintang was in the ascendancy
in China, Overseas Chinese were enlisted in Chinese national campaigns and pressured to make financial contributions
to Chinese causes. They were encouraged to retain their
Chinese culture by attending local Chinese schools (if they
were unable to return to China for their education), learning
the national Chinese language (kuo yu), and adhering to
Chinese customs and traditions. Locally published Chinese
newspapers kept them better informed about developments
in China than about events in the countries of their resi-
dence. Chinese secret societies and political parties established branches among them. In the first few years after they
came to power in China, the Communists, competing with
the Kuomintang for influence among the Overseas Chinese,
followed essentially the same policy of binding them to
China.

The situation in the Overseas Chinese community in
Rangoon as I found it in 1950-51 when I served there as the
first Chinese-language officer in the American Embassy
illustrates the extent to which these communities were
oriented towards China. Like most large Chinese communities in Southeast Asian urban centers, the one in Rangoon
was organized along many different lines. A local Chinese
resident might belong to a half-dozen or so societies, each
representing a different aspect of his identity and from each
of which he might derive some assistance in time of need.
Typically, the societies to which he belonged might include
his family name organization; a society of persons having

the same place of origin in China; a craft guild or business association; an alumni association of the local Chinese school he attended; a quasi-religious organization or benevolent association; and possibly a branch of a Chinese secret society or political party. Most of these organizations would be affiliated with similar ones in other parts of Southeast Asia.

Only a minority of the Chinese in Rangoon at that time seemed to be politically aligned; the majority tried to steer clear of political involvement. But few could escape the consequences of the vast upheaval which had taken place in China. A constant battle raged between local Kuomintang and Communist partisans for control of Chinese community organizations, especially the schools. In general the Kuomintang seemed to have more strength among the Cantonese, while the Communists were stronger among the people from Amoy, who slightly outnumbered the Cantonese. The reasons for this political split among place-of-origin lines (which happened also to be along linguistic lines) boiled down to a follow-my-leader outlook on the part of the local Chinese. A prominent Singapore businessman long recognized as the leader of Amoy organizations in Southeast Asia had been conspicuously pro-Peking in his pronouncements, and this had influenced the views of the Amoy group among Rangoon Overseas Chinese. On the other hand, the local Kuomintang organization was run by Cantonese.

The four Chinese newspapers published in Rangoon at that time roughly corresponded to political divisions within the community. Two were fence-straddling, while the other two were strongly partisan. One of these was the organ of the Burmese branch of the Kuomintang; the other, appropriately named *Jen Min Jih Pao* [People's Daily] was thoroughly Communist. The latter, I was startled to discover after reading it for some weeks, carried news stories of purported

Burmese Communist insurgent victories over the Burmese army filed from insurgent headquarters. No Burmese or local English-language newspaper could have gotten away with this.

The Burmese government appeared to be largely indifferent to political activities within the Chinese community, or to what was carried in the Chinese newspapers. This attitude probably resulted from a combination of ignorance and a reluctance to offend the PRC, with which Burma had just established diplomatic relations. Some years later, however, the Burmese government did crack down on Chinese schools, newspapers, and other informational activites.[90]

The open support which the Rangoon *Jen Min Jih Pao* gave to the Burmese Communist insurgents was consistent with Peking's hard-line foreign policy of the time, and with its use of Overseas Chinese to support Communist movements in countries where they resided.[91]

Major Chinese policy statements during this period were militant in tone and suggested that Peking might use the Overseas Chinese as a fifth column.[92] One such pronouncement on New Year's Day, 1950, by the chief of the Overseas Chinese Commission, Ho Hsian-ning, called on Overseas Chinese to act as the "outer circle" of the vanguard of revolution.[93]

With the end of the Korean War came a significant shift in the PRC's foreign policy emphasis, from militant support of revolution to cultivation of state relations, especially with Asian and African countries. At about the same time Peking made an important change in its policy toward Overseas Chinese. Speaking to the First National People's Congress in September 1954, Premier Chou En-lai asked the Overseas Chinese to respect the laws and customs of the countries in which they lived. He also offered to settle the question of dual citizenship. Peking thus signaled its willingness to modify the nationality policy Chinese governments had embraced for decades. In April 1955, during the Afro-Asian Conference at Bandung, President Sukarno of Indonesia and Premier Chou En-lai signed a treaty in which the PRC agreed that it would no longer regard as Chinese citizens Overseas Chinese in Indonesia who opted for Indonesian citizenship. China offered to negotiate similar treaties with other countries but found no takers. Later Peking modified its policy so as to eliminate the need for a formal international agreement before Chinese abroad could acquire the citizenship of another country.[94]

A further change in Chinese policy was revealed in 1956 when Premier Chou urged Overseas Chinese in Burma not only to respect the laws, customs, habits, and religions of the Burmese, but to intermarry with them, become Burmese citizens and, if they did so, to refrain from further involvement in Overseas Chinese organizations. Those who retained Chinese citizenship he urged either to refrain from politics or go back to China.[95] This advice was proclaimed to those who lived elsewhere in the following year when Overesas Chinese Affairs Commission Chairman Ho Hsiang-ning announced that the Chinese government "advocated" that Overseas Chinese choose the nationality of the countries where they reside.[96] Although such policies of the Overseas Chinese Affairs Commission were bitterly denounced by the radicals during the Cultural Revolution, they have been restored since 1971.[97]

The major obstacles now are to be found in the policies of the Southeast Asian governments toward the Overseas Chinese. In the atmosphere of intense nationalism that has pervaded most Southeast Asian countries since World War II, resident aliens have not been welcome and discriminatory regulations have been promulgated to limit their economic activities. Since the vast majority of aliens residing in

Southeast Asia are Chinese, such regulations are seen to be
anti-Chinese. Moreover, it has been very difficult in most
countries for Overseas Chinese to become naturalized citizens so that they could escape the discriminatory legislation
against aliens. In some cases Overseas Chinese are subjected
to official discrimination even after they become citizens. For
example, there are Filipino laws which give natural-born
citizens certain economic benefits not available to naturalized citizens.[98]

Despite the political and economic disabilities under
which they live and work, Overseas Chinese in Southeast
Asia have survived and many have prospered. Those who
have prospered have usually been highly adept at circum-
venting regulations designed to limit alien economic activity. In Thailand, for example, where such regulations are an
old story, Overseas Chinese have been able to predominate in
commerce by allowing "the top government officials a piece
of the action," to use the words of a Western observer, who
goes on point out: "A highly successful accommodation has
evolved. Government officials sit on the boards of directors
of private enterprises, and Chinese serve as management in
the state enterprises and government monopolies originally
established to keep some economic activity out of Chinese
hands."[99]

Many Overseas Chinese prospered in Burma, too, despite
nationalistic laws discriminating against them and other
aliens, until they were hit by the "Burmese Way to Socialism." Introduced by the Revolutionary Council under General Ne Win, which came to power by a coup d'état on March
2, 1962, this anticapitalist ideology dealt Burma's Overseas
Chinese, a community of petty capitalists (along with a few
major ones), a well-nigh fatal blow. By nationalizing banking, commerce, and industry, the Revolutionary Council
took away their principal means of livelihood.

Additionally, the cultural and political conformity that the Burmese Way to Socialism forced on the country's residents further undermined the Chinese community. When I returned to Burma for a second tour in 1971 it was hard to find "Chinatown" in Rangoon. Most of the Chinese store signs, once so prominently featured, were painted over; all but a few of the older residents were wearing Burmese clothes. Gone were the Chinese schools and newspapers, the political activity, and much of the cultural activity of twenty years earlier.

On the basis of my observations in Burma it is hard not to conclude that "socialism" is the greatest stimulus yet found in Southeast Asia to rapid integration of the Overseas Chinese with the local society. This should not be surprising, of course, since it was under conditions of free enterprise (as well as colonialism) that these communities originally expanded and prospered.

But as long as substantial, identifiable communities of Overseas Chinese exist, they are capable of affecting relations between China and Southeast Asian countries, even those under some form of socialist government. Thus, for example, in June 1967 demonstrations in Rangoon by Overseas Chinese youths wearing forbidden Mao buttons and chanting Cultural Revolution slogans sparked anti-Chinese riots. These in turn led to a sharp deterioration in Sino-Burmese state relations. Similar occurrences in Rangoon today would not produce such drastic repercussions because Peking's current foreign policy emphasis is on the attainment of pragmatic rather than revolutionary goals, but there is no guarantee that ideological extremists might not once again seize power in Peking, or that a chauvinistic militarist regime might not someday emerge in China. Such a Chinese government might seize upon racial riots, such as occurred in Indonesia in August 1973 and in Thailand in

July 1974, to exert strong pressure against Southeast Asian governments.

While such Chinese action seems improbable (as did the Cultural Revolution excesses), the mere existence of large, unassimilated Overseas Chinese communities makes the Southeast Asian countries in which they exist vulnerable to pressure from China. Southeast Asian leaders worry about this vulnerability, and such worries helped to delay normalization of state relations with the PRC. This was made quite clear, for example, in a speech given by the Malaysian minister of home affairs and internal security affairs to the Pacific investment conference in Singapore in the fall of 1973, in which he asked the PRC to "dovetail" its own laws and policies affecting people of the Chinese race living in Southeast Asia "with the requirements of the present situation."[100]

Malaysia and Singapore, of course, are particularly sensitive to the question of China's relationship with the Overseas Chinese. Because of Malaysia's huge Chinese minority (about 34 percent in the country as a whole and 50 percent in West Malaysia), its very survival depends upon racial harmony between Malays and Chinese. The two races have shared political power since Malayan independence, but not all Chinese are satisfied that their share is large enough. Thus the main opposition parties as well as the Communist "terrorists" are predominantly Chinese. In short, opportunities abound in Malaysia for Peking to exploit its racial and ideological bonds with political dissidents in both the public sphere and underground.

In Singapore the problem is somewhat different, since the Overseas Chinese dominate the politics and culture of the country as well as its economy. Singapore is nevertheless affected by the wariness of its Southeast Asian neighbors towards the Overseas Chinese. It is careful to maintain the appearance of a multiracial state and to emphasize its own nationalism as distinct from Chinese nationalism. But just because it is predominantly a Chinese country, Singapore is especially susceptible to the PRC's racial/national appeal.

When Malaysia and the PRC established diplomatic relations in May 1974, the joint communiqué issued by their prime ministers dealt with the Overseas Chinese problem among other things, but it revealed nothing new in China's policy. Both countries rejected dual nationality, as the PRC had done long before. China declared that it considered anyone of Chinese origin who had freely taken Malaysian nationality as having automatically forfeited Chinese nationality. Those who retained Chinese nationality were enjoined to abide by the laws and respect the customs and habits of Malaysia, and they were assured that "their proper rights and interests would be protected by the Government of China and respected by the Government of Malaysia."[101] Unmentioned in the communiqué was the status of over 200,000 stateless inhabitants of Malaysia of Chinese race; neither the PRC nor Malaysia seemed anxious to extend citizenship to them.[102] Thus the establishment of diplomatic relations between Kuala Lumpur and Peking has not solved the Overseas Chinese problem, but it has provided a channel of communication between the two governments which could be helpful in preventing this problem from becoming a serious irritant in their relations.

From the political standpoint the Overseas Chinese communities in Southeast Asia have, on balance, been a liability to the PRC. Recognition of this fact presumably lay behind the shift in Peking's policy toward the Overseas Chinese in the mid-1950s, and hopefully it will keep Peking on its present course of encouraging them to become naturalized in their countries of domicile. For their part, Southeast Asian nationals can make an essential contribution to this process

by adopting nationality laws and economic policies that
expedite rather than hinder the assimilation of their Overseas Chinese populations. The normalization of state relations with the PRC has apparently helped the Philippines
and Thailand recognize the importance of such measures.[103]

4

The Economic Factor

Not so long ago the food and energy resources of Southeast Asia were thought to offer a tempting target for a China hard pressed to feed its growing population and seriously short of oil. Writing in the mid-1960s, an American authority on China's economy expressed the view that the integration of Southeast Asia with the economy of China "would certainly solve China's acute fuels problem and could fully emancipate her from dependence on the Soviet Union for raw materials or on the West for grain."[104] Whatever the merits of this idea may have been ten years ago, it is clearly not valid today. China no longer has an "acute fuels problem" but rather a rapidly growing exportable surplus of oil, and it has been able to cope successfully with its food problem without Southeast Asian grain. In fact, China has exported substantial quantities of grain to that region.

China today is potentially one of the world's largest oil producers and exporters. The Chinese believe they have the third largest proven reserves in the world and hope to produce 400 million tons of oil in 1980.[104] While there may be some question whether this goal can be achieved unless China is willing "to tolerate foreign involvement in the development of its oil industry,"[106] there is no question that the PRC's production and export of oil will continue to grow rapidly and play a significant role in its foreign trade. China's exports of crude oil began in 1973 with a sale of 1 million tons to Japan. In 1974 exports to non-Communist countries exceeded 4.5 million tons and earned the PRC approximately $450 million.[107] In 1975 Japan alone contracted to buy 8 million tons, which should have earned China some $600 million.[108] At these prices the projected export to Japan of 40 million tons of oil in 1980 would bring the PRC some $3 billion, or more than double its earnings from all its exports to Japan combined in 1974. Such earnings will enable China to eliminate its foreign trade deficit[106] and expand its imports of plants and equipment essential to the achievement of its industrial growth goals.

Not only has China's oil bonanza removed Southeast Asia as a potential target of Chinese military expansion for the sake of oil, but it has even provided the opportunity for Peking to export small quantities of oil to Thailand and the Philippines. For the present, however, the political symbolism of the PRC's gesture of making oil available at a time when the two countries were feeling the pinch of the energy crisis is more significant than its portent for trade. Chinese oil exported to these countries has a high wax content which has limited its usefulness. In fact, the Thai government is reported to have suspended all deals involving Chinese oil.[110]

The PRC's limitations as supplier of oil to Southeast Asia

may be less significant in the long run than its competition with Southeast Asia as an exporter of oil to world markets. Already Indonesia is feeling the pinch of Chinese rivalry for its principal oil market, Japan. While exports of Indonesian oil to Japan slumped 6 percent in 1974 as compared with the previous year, those of Chinese oil quadrupled. In an effort to expand their oil exports to Japan still further in 1975, the Chinese reduced their prices from $12.80 per barrel to $12.10, undercutting the Indonesian price of $12.60 per barrel[111] as well as the price of comparable crude from the Middle East.[112]

Other Southeast Asian countries may eventually join Indonesia (and Brunei, the second largest oil exporter in the Far East) as competitors with China in the international oil trade. Malaysia is nearing the status of oil exporter, while Burma, an exporter before World War II, hopes that offshore oil exploration now being conducted by foreign companies will enable it to achieve that status once again. Thailand and the Philippines also have hopes of significant offshore oil discoveries soon. When and how Cambodia and Vietnam will exploit their offshore oil potential is not yet clear.

Future exploration for offshore oil may exacerbate existing territorial disputes in the South China Sea involving China and various Southeast Asian countries. Chinese claims to the Paracels and other island groups in the South China Sea, such as the Spratly (or Nan Sha) Islands, date back many centuries, but Chinese authority has not been exercised over them continuously and some have been occupied by other countries. Disputed sovereignty over the Paracel Islands (or Hsi Sha as they are called by the Chinese) has already led to armed conflict. In January 1974 Chinese naval forces drove a South Vietnamese garrison off one of the Paracels, thereby gaining possession of the entire Paracel group. Islands in the Spratly group have been occupied by

North Vietnamese forces,[113] and nearby islands are claimed
by the Philippines. If the bed of the South China Sea proves
to be a storehouse of oil, as some think, disputes over the
ownership of these island groups could become a major
irritant in Sino-Southeast Asian relations.

The PRC's accomplishments in food production hardly
match the rags-to-riches story of its oil, but Peking has been
able, on the whole, to cope successfully with the gigantic
task of feeding the world's largest population.[114] In fact, an
American authority on the world food crisis has commented:
"Perhaps the most impressive gain among the developing
countries has been China's apparent achievement of an
adequate diet for its 800 million people."[115] This achievement has resulted primarily from the PRC's ability during
most of the years since its establishment in 1949 to increase
its grain production at a rate faster than that of its population growth. Thus Premier Chou En-lai told the Fourth
National People's Congress in January 1975 that "while
China's population has increased 60 percent since the liberation of the country, grain output has increased 140 percent."[116]

In terms of quantity the PRC has been a net importer of
grain since 1961, although in recent years, at least, China's
great imports and exports have been in rough balance in
terms of value.[117] By taking advantage of the difference in
price between rice and wheat on the world market, China has
been able to import more than 3 times as much grain by
volume than it exports. In 1973, for example, it sold 1.3
million tons of rice abroad and imported 6 million tons of
wheat and corn. By one calculation this exchange of rice for
wheat and corn would have enabled China to feed about 26
million more people than it could have fed without this
trade.[118]

It does not necessarily follow, however, that 26 million people would have starved in the absence of grain imports in 1973. The significance of these imports is, much more likely, that they permitted the Chinese to enjoy the "adequate diet" mentioned above. Such an explanation is consistent with Chinese Vice Minister for Agriculture and Forestry Hao Chung-shih's statement to the Rome World Food Conference that "China does not rely on imports for feeding her population. The main purpose of our imports is to change some food varieties."[119] Another purpose might be to increase China's food stocks in accordance with Chairman Mao's teaching: "Dig tunnels deep, store grain everywhere and never seek hegemony."[120]

In view of previous fears that Southeast Asia's "rice bowl" might tempt a food-deficient PRC into adventurist policies, that region's actual contribution to meeting China's food needs is instructive. Instead of supplying rice to China, Southeast Asia has in recent years been a net importer of rice from China, and this has helped to pay for the wheat imports that have provided China with an extra margin of food. Thus it has been the rice-deficit countries of Southeast Asia, such as Singapore and Indonesia, that have made the most valuable contribution to meeting China's food problem, rather than the rice-exporting countries such as Thailand and Burma. In short, what the PRC needs from Southeast Asia more than its rice is foreign exchange—something that cannot be gained by conquest. The PRC regularly enjoys net earnings of foreign exchange from its trade and usually from each of its trading partners in Southeast Asia. Malaysia and Singapore are China's largest trading partners in the Third World. In 1973 the PRC's trade surplus with these two nations and Indonesia amounted to $335 million,[121] and in 1974 it had grown to $425 million.[122] Because China's trade has a high degree of multilateralism, the export surpluses it

accumulates in its trade with Southeast Asia help to finance
the imports of plants and equipment it needs from Japan
and the West.[123] With the expansion of state relations
between the PRC and countries of Southeast Asia, Sino–
Southeast Asian trade should continue to increase to the
mutual benefit of China and the countries of the region.

Remittances to China from Overseas Chinese in Southeast
Asia have been an important supplement to the PRC's
foreign exchange earnings. It is virtually impossible to
measure the volume of these remittances accurately and
estimates vary widely,[124] but even on the basis of the lowest
estimates it may be concluded that during the past twenty-
five years such remittances have brought hundreds of millions of dollars' worth of foreign exchange to the PRC. The
Overseas Chinese have also contributed to China's foreign
exchange earnings by their consumption of Chinese foodstuffs and manufactured goods. At the same time, because of
their important role in the commerce of Southeast Asian
countries, Overseas Chinese have undoubtedly boosted the
sales of such commodities to the peoples of these countries.
Indeed, food and light industrial products make up China's
principal exports to Southeast Asia. But as Overseas Chinese
communities become assimilated over the coming years their
ties with China are bound to diminish, and likewise their
contributions to China's foreign exchange earnings.

Until 1974 the PRC had provided economic assistance at
one time or another to all the Southeast Asian countries with
which it had established state relations, i.e., Burma, Cambodia, Indonesia, Laos, and North Vietnam. Although there is
no indication as yet that Peking has begun economic assistance to the countries of the region with which it has more
recently established diplomatic relations, such a policy
would be consistent with its past practices.

Peking's aid to the non-Communist governments of

Southeast Asia has characteristically been much affected by the ebb and flow of political tides. About six months after the abortive PKI coup in Indonesia, Peking terminated its aid program there with the bulk of its funds still unexpended. Its aid program in Burma was suspended in 1967 at the request of the Burmese government and restored in 1971 by mutual agreement. After Prince Sihanouk's ouster in 1970, Peking cut off aid to the Cambodian government in Phnom Penh but apparently continued it to Sihanouk's government-in-exile.[125] Peking's major economic aid project in Laos was the construction of roads but, as already noted, despite the fact that the original agreement was made with the government in Vientiane, these roads were all built in Pathet Lao territory and the project was expanded far beyond that agreed to by Vientiane. Other projects concluded between Peking and Vientiane in December 1963 were apparently never completed.[126] However, following the reestablishment of the coalition government in Laos, China again offered aid to Vientiane.[127]

The PRC provides economic aid to developing countries on terms more generous than those offered by any other major aid donor. Since 1960, its aid loans have been free of interest. Formerly such loans were repayable in ten years following a grace period of ten years, but in recent years grace periods have been extended to twenty or thirty years, with longer amortization periods than before.[128] Another attractive feature of China's economic assistance is that Chinese technicians and workers are paid in accordance with the standards of the receiving country. One student of Chinese economic aid estimates that this feature makes Chinese aid worth about 35 percent more to the receiving country than aid in the same numerical amount provided by other countries.[129]

While economic assistance from the PRC may be the

cheapest available to Third World countries, it also has some drawbacks. During my 1971-73 tour in Burma, where more Chinese aid expenditures have been made than in any other non-Communist Southeast Asian country, I heard three main complaints from knowledgeable Burmese and foreign sources: (1) that the industrial plants built with such aid (e.g., textile and paper mills) were technologically not up to date; (2) that the entire aid program moved very slowly; and (3) that the number of personnel assigned to individual projects was considerably larger than the number assigned to comparable projects by Japanese and Western countries. There were also hints that the Chinese had suggested certain road and railroad projects which the Burmese turned down for security reasons. Nevertheless, there was no indication of basic dissatisfaction with the Chinese aid program on the part of the Burmese, and it had obviously made a contribution to Burma's economic development.

To sum up, the economic factor is not of vital importance (which is perhaps fortunate), but it is generally a positive element in Sino–Southeast Asian relations. Trade is mutually beneficial and should continue to grow, providing the PRC with the foreign exchange it needs to finance imports from the industrialized countries. In a world faced with dwindling energy supplies, competition in the world oil export market should not prove detrimental to either side in the long run. Chinese economic aid and technical assistance could be useful to most Southeast Asian nations but will probably continue to be concentrated on the Indo-Chinese states and Burma.

5

Third-Power Policies

More important to the relations between Southeast Asia and China than Communist insurgency, Overseas Chinese, or the economic factor are the policies of the superpowers, the United States and the Soviet Union. Shifts in the relationships between the PRC and the Soviet Union and the PRC and the United States have profoundly affected Sino-Southeast Asian relations in the past few years. Japan's enormous economic impact on Southeast Asia must also be taken into consideration in any assessment of the influence of third powers on these relations. Thus, Japan is of considerably greater economic importance to Southeast Asia and to China than are Southeast Asia and China to each other.

The establishment of diplomatic relations between Thailand and the PRC (and between the Philippines and the PRC) in mid-1975 was not a panicky reaction to the sudden collapse of South Vietnam and the fall of Phnom Penh, but rather the almost inevitable consequence of the changed relationship between the United States and the PRC dating from President Nixon's visit to China in February 1972. As Thai Prime Minister Kukrit Pramoj pointed out in Peking on June 30, 1975, his visit there was "the result of the development of relations between Thailand and the People's Republic of China that have progressed step by step over the recent years."[130] When the United States adopted a posture of détente toward the PRC, its allies in SEATO were bound to follow suit. Their course of action was greatly facilitated by Peking's own post–Cultural Revolution policy of emphasizing state relations and by its seating in the United Nations in the autumn of 1971.

The changed relationship between the United States and the PRC which so affected Sino–Southeast Asian relations was in turn largely (though not entirely) due to the severe deterioration in Sino-Soviet relations following the armed border clashes between the two nations in the winter of 1969. These clashes and subsequent A-bomb rattling by Soviet propagandists brought home to Peking its military vulnerability. Judging by the private reactions of PRC representatives in Hong Kong (where I was serving as consul general) Peking was genuinely worried about the possibility of a Soviet attack. The campaigns which were launched throughout China to dig air-raid shelters and store grain reflected this concern.

When Edgar Snow visited China in the fall of 1970, he found that Mao, who had refused to send any message to President Johnson in 1965, was now willing to talk to President Nixon. This willingness was due in part to the Chinese perception that the United States, deeply divided over the war in Vietnam, wanted to withdraw from it and needed to come to an understanding with China.[131] But

Mao's change of heart was also due to Peking's serious concern over the Soviet threat. As Snow observed: "Very high among the reasons why Sino-American rapprochement interested China was to improve her strategic position in dealing with Russia."[132]

The threat of Soviet power to China is still the major preoccupation of Chinese foreign policy. Peking genuinely fears Soviet encirclement. Thus, already confronted with Soviet armed forces a million strong on their northern borders,[133] the Chinese have become especially sensitive to any evidence of Soviet expansion on their southern frontiers. For this reason the Indian subcontinent and the Indian Ocean have long been a focus of Chinese concern. Now Peking sees Southeast Asia as also vulnerable to the Soviet Union's "wild ambitions," to use the words of Vice Premier Teng in his speech of welcome to Thai Prime Minister Kukrit Pramoj.

Ironically, Chinese apprehension on this score has grown in the wake of the Communist triumph in Indochina. Chinese denunciations of the Soviet Union began to mount after the Communist victories in Vietnam and Cambodia and by July 1975 had reached their most sustained level since the armed clashes on the Sino-Soviet border in 1969. Many of the Chinese accusations were "aimed at what was described as Soviet expansion in Southeast Asia."[134] It is indeed a striking reflection of the changed relationships in Southeast Asia that final Communist victory in Vietnam, to which the PRC contributed heavily in arms, materials, and even man-power, should have enhanced Chinese security worries rather than calmed them.

The PRC's worries have been particularly focused on Vietnam. Peking has been concerned that Hanoi, which during the Vietnam war was careful to keep on good terms with both Moscow and Peking, is tilting towards the Soviet

Union. Although the PRC's fears that the Soviet Union had obtained Hanoi's consent to use the formerly American naval base at Cam Ranh Bay in South Vietnam were apparently unfounded,[135] the Soviet presence in South Vietnam after the Communist victory did seem to completely overshadow the PRC's. [136] Moreover, Hanoi has appeared to lean toward Moscow on some issues that have divided China and the Soviet Union. Thus, in a joint communiqué signed by Le Duan and Leonid Brezhnev in Moscow in November 1975, Hanoi supported Soviet positions on détente and the Helsinki Conference on European Security, positions strongly opposed by Peking. Presumably in return for economic aid supplied by the Soviet Union and Eastern European members of COMECON, Hanoi also seems bent on following Soviet rather than Chinese patterns.[137]

Hanoi's tilt towards Moscow is particularly dangerous for China because it provides an opportunity for the Soviet Union to exploit the clashes of interest between Hanoi and Peking. The most conspicuous of these is the dispute, described earlier in connection with potential conflict over petroleum resources, over the Paracel and Spratly island groups in the South China Sea. This dispute may also have strategic importance in Peking's eyes—at least enough importance to produce an anxious Chinese wish to deny the islands to Soviet naval use. Soviet propaganda has not lessened such Chinese apprehension nor improved Sino-Vietnamese relations by supporting Hanoi's claim to the Paracels and by calling China's seizure of them "aggression against the Vietnamese people."[138]

The most serious conflict of interest between Peking and Hanoi, however, may arise not from territorial disputes but from Hanoi's ambitions in Southeast Asia. Though it is not apparent how far these extend, they probably include domination of Indochina if not of other parts of Southeast Asia.

Aside from the leadership which Vietnamese have long asserted in the Indo-Chinese Communist movement, Hanoi provided assistance essential to the eventual victory of Communist forces in Laos and Cambodia. It would be only natural for Hanoi to wish to continue its predominant position now that its prolonged efforts and great sacrifices have achieved success throughout Indochina.

Hanoi's influence is particularly strong in Laos, where its military participation on the side of the Pathet Lao was unquestionably decisive in the latter's ultimate success. Furthermore, the continued presence of some 30,000 North Vietnamese troops in Laos, even after the reestablishment of the coalition government in Vientiane and the withdrawal of the American and Thai military presence,[139] undoubtedly hastened the complete takeover of the country by the Pathet Lao, and the subsequent abolition of the coalition government and 600-year-old Lao monarchy in December 1975.[140]

In February 1976 the new prime minister of the fledgling People's Democratic Republic of Laos journeyed to Hanoi together with other representatives of the Laotian government and Communist Party to confer with their North Vietnamese opposite numbers on the subject of strengthening economic and cultural links between the two countries. Of particular interest to Laos' neighbors, China and Thailand, may have been the discussion of the construction of an all-weather road designed to link Laos to a Vietnamese port, which would reduce Laos' dependence on transit facilities through Thailand for its imports and exports.[141] Indicative, perhaps, of Hanoi's leadership aspirations in Indochina was the promise contained in the joint communiqué issued following Prime Minister Kaysone Phomvihan's visit to Hanoi that the two sides would work together "to increase solidarity between Laos, Cambodia and Vietnam and to destroy imperialism entirely."[142]

Whatever Hanoi's aspirations may be for hegemony over Indochina, however, they are more likely to be frustrated in Cambodia than in Laos. Although the Khmer Rouge victors in Cambodia also owe much to North Vietnamese assistance, they have rather conspicuously praised Peking for its support, and, from the time they assumed power in Phnom Penh, China has been the paramount foreign presence in Cambodia. The first high-level delegation from the new Cambodian government to go abroad went to Peking. According to a joint Sino-Cambodian communiqué issued on August 19, 1975, this mission resulted in a Chinese promise of economic aid to Cambodia and a public endorsement by the Cambodians of the Chinese line on major international issues.[143]

While Cambodia's new government appears to have given priority to its relations with China, it has also established relations with Hanoi, and some of its most powerful members are considered to be pro-Hanoi in outlook.[144] Both by reason of its geographical propinquity and of its long ties with Cambodian Communists, Hanoi will be a formidable rival to Peking for influence in Phnom Penh. The Soviet government, on the other hand, has been ostracized by the Khmer Rouge government.

While it would seem to be a reasonable presumption under any circumstances that the PRC would not favor a dominating role for Hanoi in Indochina, let alone in the rest of Southeast Asia, given the present Chinese fear of Soviet encirclement Peking would be especially loath to see a Moscow-leaning Hanoi play such a role. On the other hand, the Soviet Union might see such a role for Hanoi as a useful block to the extension of Chinese influence in the area. Thus Moscow is believed to support Hanoi's desire for an all-Indochina conference while Peking does not.[145] The phenomenal growth of the Soviet presence in Laos[146] strengthens

Hanoi's influence there, while the Soviet Union's exclusion from Cambodia helps give Peking an edge over Hanoi there. Moreover, the establishment of diplomatic ties and economic accords between Cambodia and Thailand, apparently with Peking's blessing if not by its arrangement, also undermines whatever hegemonial aspirations Hanoi may have with respect to Cambodia.

Although Vietnam's propinquity to China inevitably puts some restraint on the extent to which Hanoi can challenge its giant neighbor, Sino-Soviet hostility provides Hanoi with a certain maneuverability to press its own interests against Peking's, a maneuverability enhanced by its victory in the Vietnam war. Egged on by a Soviet policy aimed at keeping Chinese influence in check, Hanoi might be tempted to pursue hegemonistic aims within Indochina if not beyond.

The Soviet Union served notice more than six years ago that it would take an interest in post–Vietnam war security problems in Southeast Asia. At a conference of Workers and Communist parties in Moscow in June 1969, Soviet Communist Party Secretary General Leonid Brezhnev floated a vague proposal for Asian collective security.[147] This proposal, based on an assumption of declining American power in Asia, was not followed up systematically for several years and seemed to be more of a trial balloon than a serious diplomatic initiative. However, in March 1972 Brezhnev revived the proposal and fleshed it out in a speech to the Congress of Trade Unions. It was probably not mere coincidence that Brezhnev's elaboration of the Asian collective security idea came soon after President Nixon's visit to China and the publication of the Nixon-Chou communiqué in Shanghai. In any case, the new version of the Brezhnev proposal contained wording much like some of that in the Shanghai communiqué; it encompassed the ubiquitous five principles of peaceful coexistence first put forth by Chou and Nehru.

In the following year further additions were made to the Asian collective security concept to make it more appealing to Third World countries. Thus Soviet Premier Kosygin was reported to have told Iranian Prime Minister Hoveyda on August 8 that the concept included self-determination of every people, impermissibility of annexation through aggression, peaceful settlement of international disputes, the inalienable right to sovereign possession of natural resources, and implementation of socioeconomic reforms.[148] Shortly afterward in a speech at Alma Ata in Khazakstan, near the Chinese border, Brezhnev emphasized that the Soviet Union advocated equal participation of all Asian countries without exception in the proposed collective security system.

Made at an apparently carefully chosen site, this further elaboration of the collective security proposal was obviously designed to reassure Peking. From the beginning the PRC has seen the Brezhnev proposal as an anti-China ploy and has vociferously opposed it. This is not surprising, considering that it was first put forward when Sino-Soviet tension was at its height and in an international forum where Brezhnev had strongly denounced the PRC. In attacking the proposal, Peking has stressed its dangers to other countries. For example, in what was the PRC's maiden appearance at an Economic Commission for Asia and the Far East (ECAFE) meeting, its representative, An Chih-yuan, declared on April 12, 1973 that the USSR's "immediate aim in energetically advocating 'Asian collective security' is to control and divide Asian countries and incorporate them gradually into its sphere of influence." He predicted that "such a system can only bring new disasters to the people of Asia."[149]

The assurances contained in Brezhnev's Alma Ata speech

did not perceptibly alter Peking's propaganda line. In a
typical attack, a *Peking Review* article published December
28, 1973, called the proposed Asian collective security system
"in fact a system of aggression and expansion," and accused
the Soviet Union of wanting "to replace the United States
and exercise hegemony in Asia, that is, to 'fill the vacuum'
there."[150] This Chinese apprehension concerning Soviet
aims may not be far off the mark. The perceived purpose of
Moscow's collective security scheme does seem to be to
ensure that the Soviet Union rather than the PRC will fill
any void left by the decline of American power in Southeast
Asia.[151]

However, the Soviet Union has so far met with little
success in gathering support for its collective security system. No Southeast Asian government has endorsed the idea,
although some leaders have made polite noises about it. For
example, Malaysian Prime Minister Razak said during a
visit to Moscow on October 3, 1972, that since the proposal
was based on "peaceful coexistence" and "noninterference," it was in harmony with the neutralization
concept of the Association of Southeast Asian Nations
(ASEAN); Indonesian Prime Minister Malik was reported to
have said in Jakarta on March 16, 1974, that Indonesia did
not want to "refuse the Soviet collective security proposal"
but he felt that more information on the idea was still
needed.[152] It is difficult to conceive, however, of any Southeast Asian country giving substantial support to the Asian
collective security proposal or any other Soviet-sponsored
security system adamantly opposed by the PRC.

The ASEAN countries (Indonesia, Malaysia, the Philippines, Thailand, and Singapore) have a proposal of their
own for ensuring Southeast Asian independence. This
proposal, put forward by the ASEAN foreign ministers at
their meeting in Kuala Lumpur on November 27, 1971, calls

for international "recognition of and respect for Southeast
Asia as a Zone of Peace, Freedom, and Neutrality, free from
any form or manner of interference by outside powers."[153]
Although the details of how this proposal will be implemented have not been worked out, Peking has apparently
endorsed the concept. Thus in his June 30 speech in Peking,
Prime Minister Kukrit Pramoj asserted that "the Government of Thailand warmly welcomes the pronouncements of
the Government of the People's Republic of China in
support of the ASEAN and of the desire of ASEAN countries
to see Southeast Asia a zone of peace, freedom and neutrality."

Despite its failure to attract Southeast Asian support, the
Soviet proposal for an Asian collective security system
remains an important vehicle for Soviet policy in the region.
Following the European security conference held in Helsinki in August 1975, for example, Soviet propaganda organs
gave renewed attention to the "extremely urgent" need for an
Asian collective security system.[154] From the standpoint of
the ASEAN states, even though they shy away from endors-
ing the Brezhnev proposal, it does symbolize Soviet interest
in the region which for them is a useful balance to China's
interest.

Soviet interest has also served to split the extreme left in
non-Communist Southeast Asian countries, which has been
useful to their governments. For example, in Burma, which
has had diplomatic relations with both the Soviet Union and
the PRC for two and a half decades, the far left political
opposition has long been split into pro-Moscow and pro-
Peking factions. The Peking-dominated Communist insurgency has thereby been deprived of the solid support it might
have otherwise received from the Burmese radical left. Since
its abortive coup in September 1967 the Peking-oriented PKI
in Indonesia has been badly splintered and a pro-Moscow

faction has developed, weakening the comeback efforts of the PKI. In the Philippines pro-Moscow Communist insurgents, who had been constantly harassed by pro-Peking Communist insurgents, surrendered to the government in the fall of 1974, pledging peaceful cooperation, while the pro-Peking faction continued its armed rebellion.

Thus certain advantages can accrue to the ASEAN countries and to Burma from the Sino-Soviet rivalry, but this rivalry could also pose a great danger to them if Southeast Asia becomes a major arena in the Sino-Soviet global struggle. The fact that both Communist powers operate at the covert level of direct support to political factions and insurgent groups as well as at the conventional diplomatic level heightens this danger. In short, the security interests of Southeast Asian countries could suffer severely in the course of an intensified Sino-Soviet struggle.

In contrast to Soviet policies, which mainly affect the security aspects of Sino–Southeast Asian relations, Japan's policies have their principal impact in the economic field. Because of Japan's decision to renounce war and limit its armed forces to those necessary for defense of its home territory, Japan menaces neither Southeast Asia nor China as it once did. By concentrating on its economic growth and the development of its international trade instead of attempting to regain its prewar military might, Japan has benefited China and the Southeast Asian countries as well as itself.

Bereft of any political or military power with which to pressure its trading partners, Japan has had to achieve its preeminence in their trade by offering them more advantageous terms than they could get anywhere else. In fact, since emotional prejudices left over from World War II militated against these countries trading with Japan, the economic benefits of such business had to be even more appealing than would otherwise have been the case.[155] Thus if the PRC and the Southeast Asian countries have judged their economic self-interest correctly, they, as well as Japan, have profited greatly from their trading relationships.

Nevertheless, Japan's economic prominence in some Southeast Asian countries has spawned fears of Japanese economic domination and has even led to violent anti-Japanese demonstrations. But such countries have it within their sovereign power to limit Japan's economic relations with them if they feel threatened. Indonesia did just this following the anti-Japanese riots sparked by the visit there of Premier Tanaka in January 1974. President Suharto laid down new restrictions on foreign economic activity which primarily affected the Japanese.[156]

The chance that Japan will again seek domination of Southeast Asia by military means seems remote. Despite perennial fears abroad of a revival of Japanese militarism, there is no sign in Japan of popular support for rearmament or for the concepts, such as Japan's "divine mission," by which the Japanese rationalized their conquests of the 1930s and 1940s.[157] The economic incentives which made an expansionist policy seem feasible to Japanese nationalists in pre–World War II days have almost disappeared. Japan's dependence on imported raw materials, energy, and food, has grown so enormously since those days that the resources of the territories included in the old East Asian Co-Prosperity Sphere are no longer adequate to meet its require-ments.[158]

Moreover, instead of facing a weak and divided China as it did then, Japan now must deal with a unified China armed with nuclear weapons. With its heavy concentration of population and industry in a comparatively small area, Japan is especially vulnerable to nuclear warfare. Instead of facing colonial Southeast Asian governments weakened by nationalist independence movements bent on overthrowing them, Japan now must deal with independent countries whose governments represent those very nationalist movements. In short, political, economic, and strategic circumstances today could hardly differ more from those that confronted Japan when it embarked on a policy of military expansionism.

In the near future, at least, there seem to be no major conflicts of interest between the PRC and Japan in Southeast Asia. Japan in no way threatens the PRC's security interests there as Peking believes the Soviet Union does and the United States did. The PRC poses no threat to Japan's access to Southeast Asia's raw materials or to its oil supply lines running through that region. The PRC and Japan do not compete for Southeast Asian markets. The PRC exports primarily light manufactured goods and foodstuffs to them, while Japan's leading exports are steel, cars, and ships. There may be some competition between China and Japan for some Southeast Asian exports such as rubber and timber, but not for the region's principal export to Japan, mineral fuels, which accounted for nearly 40 percent of all its imports from Southeast Asia in 1974.[159] Japan's purchases of oil and other raw materials, in fact, contribute indirectly to China's favorable balance of trade with Southeast Asia.

In Communist-dominated Indochina Japan's economic role is relatively minor, but it is certain to grow and could eventually become significant. By 1974 Japan had already established itself as Hanoi's principal non-Communist trading partner, with two-way trade amounting to about $49 million. Japan imported mainly anthracite coal from North Vietnam while exporting to it steel, chemicals, textiles, and nonferrous metals. In the summer of 1975 Tokyo negotiated an economic aid agreement with Hanoi.[160]

Japan has the capacity to forge ahead of all its competitors for Vietnam's trade as it has done in the case of the PRC.

Should Hanoi adopt Peking's policy of trading wherever the best deals can be made, Japan could become Vietnam's largest trading partner too. Such a development would reduce Vietnamese dependence on the Soviet Union and the PRC.

While there is no significant clash between Japan's and China's strategic interests in Southeast Asia, there is a conflict of political interest based on their differing ideologies. This conflict is rather muted now, due to Japan's general laissez-faire posture in Southeast Asia and China's current emphasis on state relations. Yet the PRC has not abandoned its support of revolutionary movements aimed at overthrowing the region's non-Communist governments. Whatever Peking's disclaimers may be as to the assistance it renders such movements, it does assert a belief in the righteousness of their cause and a desire to see their ultimate victory. To the extent, then, that Japan's trade, aid, and investment strengthens the political status quo in Southeast Asia, Japan is helping to thwart the attainment of Peking's long-range political objectives.

The PRC's ideological conflict with Japan in Southeast Asia and elsewhere, however, takes second place to its concern with the Soviet threat. Peking is anxious to prevent this threat from growing in Northeast as well as in Southeast Asia. Thus it has been concerned about possible joint Soviet-Japanese projects for the exploitation of gas, oil, and other resources in Siberia and the other Soviet far eastern provinces, which might strengthen the Soviet Union strategically and draw Japan and the Soviet Union closer together.

Peking may also fear that Soviet-Japanese cooperation in such projects would reduce Tokyo's interest in trade with China, especially in imports of Chinese oil. Of all the countries in the world, Japan is the most important to the PRC economically. Not only has it been for some years

China's largest trading partner, but it is likely to become even more important as Japan buys more and more of China's oil. In sum, Peking's long-range political conflict of interest with Tokyo in Southeast Asia is presently outweighed by Peking's strategic and economic interest in maintaining good relations with Japan.

Though markedly less important to Sino–Southeast Asian relations than Japan, India plays a role that should not be overlooked. In some important respects its role is the opposite of Japan's. Thus, compared with Japan, India counts for little on the economic scene, but it does have common land and sea frontiers with Southeast Asia and a capability of bringing military forces directly to bear on these frontiers. Japan has no such capability.[161] India's armed forces, in contrast to Japan's, have had considerable combat experience in recent years. India's quick and decisive victory over Pakistan in 1971 demonstrated its military power, and its military potential gained new respect following the Indian explosion of a nuclear device in May 1974.

India's military significance for Southeast Asia is of course enhanced by New Delhi's close relations with Moscow. These relations are of particular concern to Peking. Preoccupied as it is by the threat of Soviet encirclement, the PRC tends to exaggerate Indian military subservience to the Soviet Union. For example, the *Peking Review* described the Indian-Soviet Treaty of August 1971 as "in reality for military alliance" and claimed that the Indian military operations against Pakistan which took place three months later were directed by "prominent Soviet figures . . . in New Delhi."[162] There is no evidence to support such claims. Nor is there any indication that India has expansionist ambitions against Southeast Asia or supports those ambitions Peking accuses Moscow of harboring. Nevertheless, Indian power is close at hand and with Soviet backing it is capable of

thrusting into Southeast Asia. On the other hand, by refus-
ing to facilitate any Soviet naval ambitions in the eastern
Indian Ocean, India can relieve Chinese anxieties and reduce
chances of a serious Sino-Soviet confrontation in Southeast
Asia.

The Southeast Asian country most vulnerable to an
intrusion of Indian military power is Burma. For years Naga
and Mizoo rebels have shuttled across the extreme northern
part of Burma to and from China, where they have received
military and political training and arms. The Indian government has suppressed but not extinguished their rebellion. More blatant use of Burmese territory by these or other
Chinese-supported Indian groups could provoke a countermove from India. On the other side of the ledger (as already
pointed out), Chinese fears of the encroachment of Soviet-
backed Indian power on Burma's western frontiers in the
wake of the Bangladesh war may have motivated Peking's
stepped-up support of Burmese Communist insurgent military operations in eastern Burma in 1971-73, despite an
ongoing Sino-Burmese rapprochement at the government-
to-government level.

To sum up the significance of third-power policies for
Sino–Southeast Asian relations, the U.S. rapprochement
with the PRC (as well as its withdrawal from Vietnam)
paved the way for its Southeast Asian allies to establish state
relations with Peking for the first time. Chinese fear of Soviet
encirclement has also contributed to the normalizing of state
relations between the PRC and Southeast Asian countries.
On the other hand, Chinese suspicions of Moscow's intentions have frustrated Soviet efforts to gain acceptance for its
scheme for an Asian collective security treaty which would
curb Chinese power and enhance its own influence in
Southeast Asia. Continued Sino-Soviet rivalry in Southeast
Asia contains the seeds of danger, especially for Sino-

Vietnamese relations. Japan's role in Southeast Asia, on the other hand, is basically nonthreatening to stable Sino–Southeast Asian relations, although in the longer run it may be seen by Peking to be detrimental to its interests. While Indian policy has not had much impact in the area as yet, India's strategic position and its military capacity give it a potential for greater influence in the future.

6

The Prospects

What are the prospects for Sino–Southeast Asian relations, in the light of the various factors discussed in the preceding chapters? The leadership struggle that rent the Chinese Communist Party for so long seemed in the first weeks after Mao's death to have been resolved in favor of the moderate faction and its policies. Once bereft of Mao's support, the radicals lost their political potency with surprising rapidity. The PLA as well as the moderates gained power at the radicals' expense. Thus following the purge of the radical leaders, two of the top four leaders in the PRC were military men.

Basic to the resurgence of the moderates after the Cultural Revolution and their quick victory over the radicals in the wake of Mao's death is China's need for the pragmatic domestic and foreign policies they have espoused. Such policies are necessary to ensure not only that the PRC can continue to feed its enormous and growing population, but also that it can meet the essential capital and technological requirements for the expansion and modernization of China's industry, especially its defense industry. Beyond this, unrest among China's industrial workers indicates that economic growth–oriented policies may also be necessary to meet their expectations of a better return for their labor.

Thus the ascendancy of the moderate group portends the continuation of substantially the same policies as those endorsed by the Fourth National People's Congress. In fact, with the weakening of the forces upholding the counter-claims of Maoist revolutionary values, economic growth and modernization priorities can be expected to dominate China's domestic and foreign policies even more than they have in the recent past. Such a trend would bode well for Sino–Southeast Asian relations.

Triumph by the radical faction in the post-Mao power struggle, on the other hand, would almost certainly have undermined Sino–Southeast Asian relations. In such a case, Peking's foreign policy emphasis would probably have shifted toward revolutionary ideology and support of Communist insurgencies, as it did during the Cultural Revolution. Judging by Red Guard attacks on the Overseas Chinese Commission at that time, it might also have resulted in Peking's adopting a more chauvinistic attitude toward the Overseas Chinese. Moreover, an increased emphasis on ideology would have almost inevitably exacerbated Sino-Soviet hostility and endangered the partial détente between Peking and Washington.

While the rapid downfall of the radical leadership following Mao's death has made the foregoing developments unlikely, the apparent increase in PLA influence in Peking could have some impact on China's foreign policies. The in-

dustrial growth and modernization necessary to satisfy the
PLA's requirements for modern armaments probably accounted for its support of the moderate faction in the post-
Mao power struggle, and will presumably constrain it to
continue such support. In foreign policy the PLA's influence might, however, be in the direction of a more narrowly
nationalistic and isolationist posture than the moderates
would otherwise adopt. But such a tendency would not be
likely to change Peking's current emphasis on normal state
relations in its dealings with Southeast Asia.

Despite its emphasis in recent years on normalization of
state relations with Southeast Asia, Peking has continued its
persistent public support of Communist revolutionary
movements there. Though this policy may be somewhat
muted in the future, it is not likely to be given up. The fear of
abandoning Southeast Asian revolutionary movements to
Soviet domination alone would be enough to ensure that the
PRC would maintain its links with them. These ties in turn
will continue to militate against the development of an
atmosphere of trust between Peking and the governments
these movements are attempting to overthrow. So long as
these governments can keep insurgency in check, however,
the normalization trend in Sino–Southeast Asian relations is
not likely to be fatally undermined.

But the ability of Southeast Asian governments to cope
with Communist insurgencies will depend more and more
on their ability to meet pressing domestic economic and
social problems. As Singapore's Foreign Minister Rajarat-
nam said on the eve of ASEAN's first summit conference
(held in Bali in February 1976), "the answer to insurgency is
only one part military to eight or nine parts economic
development."[163] Nationalism and anticolonialism, which
have been used effectively in the past by Southeast Asian
leaders to undermine their Communist opposition, no

longer have quite the political potency they once did. The younger generation, which has not experienced the struggle for independence from colonial rule, is more interested in how its leaders meet today's economic and social problems than in the past glories of the struggle for independence. Food, jobs, and ethnic frictions are now the overriding issues which Southeast Asian governments must meet. As the ratio of population to land becomes less and less favorable from year to year these problems become more and more pressing and difficult to solve.

For the balance of this decade, however, the non-Communist governments of Southeast Asia appear to have the resources to deal with these problems, at least effectively enough to prevent dissident revolutionary forces from coming within striking distance of seizing national power. The most vulnerable may be Burma, whose economy has been virtually stagnant for several years. While Burma has survived some twenty-seven years of insurgency of different varieties, the sheer ineptitude of the government's handling of the economy and the extent of its political repression raise serious questions regarding its survivability over the next few years. The danger is not so much from a Communist takeover, which is problematical, but that the "Union of Burma" might break up, tempting China and India to indirect intervention.

The Overseas Chinese communities in Southeast Asia will continue to give a special dimension to Sino–Southeast Asian relations, but one which will become progressively less important over time. In the short term, however, an infection of Chinese policies with an outbreak of chauvinism could stir up old fears and suspicions in Southeast Asia which recent Peking attitudes toward the Overseas Chinese have tended to allay. On the other hand, pursuit of narrowly nationalistic interests on the part of Southeast Asian nations

discriminating against Overseas Chinese, whether naturalized or alien, will also undermine progress toward integration of these communities which are capable of contributing
so much to the development of their adopted countries. In
general, the trend toward integration of these communities
into Southeast Asian polities, and the consequent diminish-
ing of their significance as an irritant in Sino–Southeast
Asian relations, is likely to continue.

As already indicated, neither China nor the Southeast
Asian countries are indispensable to one another economically. On the other hand, their economic relations are on the
whole mutually beneficial. There seems to be no reason to
believe that this equation will change. Thus, insofar as the
economic factor in Sino–Southeast Asian relations is concerned, while it is not of great significance, its influence
should continue to be exerted on the side of "normalizing"
state relations if not of strengthening them.

Peking's concern during the past few years with what it
perceives as a Soviet threat to its security has had much to do
with its willingness to accept détente with the United States
and its desire to normalize relations with Southeast Asian
nations. Peking's repeated warnings to these nations to
beware of Soviet ambitions indicate its continuing anxiety
on this score and the likelihood that PRC policy toward
Southeast Asia will continue to be affected by these perceptions.

However, the death of Mao removes the influence of his
personal animus against the Soviet Union as a factor in
Sino-Soviet relations and could pave the way to an eventual
Sino-Soviet détente. With the waning of radical strength in
Peking, the ideological conflict with the Soviet Union may
now weigh less heavily in shaping Chinese foreign policy
than it has in the past. For its part, Moscow has seen Mao as
the epitome of Chinese hostility to the Soviet Union, and his

passing may encourage it to believe in the possibility of a rapprochement with the PRC, despite early indications by the post-Mao leadership that it is not interested. Peking might come to see advantage in a modification of Sino-Soviet hostility, at least in sufficient measure to give it greater flexibility in its dealings with the United States, and perhaps with Japan.

On the other hand, a Sino-Soviet rapprochement is not likely to go to the point of active political cooperation, let alone Peking's realignment with Moscow. Territorial and other conflicts of national interest (if not of ambition) between the PRC and the Soviet Union, and the latter's inability to substitute for Japan and the West as a source of agricultural, industrial, and technological imports essential for achievement of the PRC's economic and defense goals, will limit the extent of Sino-Soviet cooperation. Thus it would not be likely to undermine the normalization of Sino–Southeast Asian state relations.

In any case, the Soviet Union's accomplishments in Southeast Asia, outside of Vietnam at least, are not particularly impressive. It does not appear to exercise significant influence in any non-Communist country, and it is difficult to conceive of any of these countries providing military bases to the Soviet Union. Even Burma, whose Burmese Way to Socialism gives it a certain ideological affinity with the Soviet Union, has been very careful not to compromise itself with the PRC by being too accommodating towards Moscow.

That the Soviet Union would move into the territory of a Southeast Asian country by main force also seems unlikely. Granted that it might have the military capability, the penalty it would pay in terms of its relations with the Third World, Japan, and the United States (and the PRC's corresponding gain) would hardly be worth the prize, for Southeast Asia is not an area of great strategic or economic importance to the Soviet Union. It is an area, however, where the Soviet Union will fish in troubled waters to cause problems for its adversaries, as it did successfully for the United States by its support of North Vietnam. At present, Sino-Vietnamese frictions may represent such troubled waters, and it is in this area that continuing Sino-Soviet rivalry may have its most disturbing effect on Sino–Southeast Asian relations.

The PRC's relations with the Communist states of Indochina are more influenced by Sino-Soviet rivalry than are its relations with their non-Communist neighbors. Although the Soviet Union appears to hold a position of influence in Vietnam and Laos superior to China's, since both of these countries have common borders with China, prudence will presumably set limits to the extent to which they lean toward the Soviet Union in the Sino-Soviet quarrel. Cambodia, on the other hand, appears to be squarely in Peking's camp, having excluded the Soviet Union from representation in Phnom Penh. There are indications of mutual Sino-Vietnamese suspicions, if not outright rivalry, which further complicate the Indo-Chinese picture.

These intra-Communist rivalries, added to the strong nationalistic tendencies manifested by the new Cambodian and Laotian Communist regimes, reduce any immediate threat, at least, that Indochina will provide a strong base for the spread of Communism into the rest of Southeast Asia. In fact, to the extent that the non-Communist countries of the region, especially those in ASEAN, can improve their economies and social conditions and strengthen their regional cooperation, they may exert an attraction for the Indo-Chinese states that will cause them to moderate their policies and will undermine any support they may be giving to Communist insurgents beyond their borders.

Moscow's propensity for stirring up trouble notwith-standing, it is unlikely that its influence will reach deep enough to disrupt relations between the PRC and any Southeast Asian country, including Vietnam. These countries are quite aware of the dangers involved in becoming entangled in the Sino-Soviet quarrel and will strive to balance their relations with the two Communist giants so as to avoid such entanglement and preserve their maneuverability. The current four-power balance in East Asia among the United States, the Soviet Union, the PRC, and Japan provides an international environment which greatly aids this process, as does the existence of a regional grouping such as ASEAN.

Thus there is reason for guarded optimism that the trend toward constructive state relations between the PRC and the non-Communist Southeast Asian countries will continue. The apparent quick triumph of the moderates with PLA backing over their radical rivals (although it may not represent the final outcome of the succession struggle) tends to allay fears that Chinese internal conflicts in the wake of Mao's death would, at best, reduce Peking's effectiveness in implementing its pragmatic foreign policies and, at worst, revive the ideological and chauvinistic extremism of the Cultural Revolution. Moreover, the growing strength of these countries (with the exception of Burma) and their cooperation in ASEAN should improve their capacities to withstand shifts in China's policies and to cope with Peking-oriented insurgencies.

In sum, while the relations of the Southeast Asian countries with China will continue to be strongly influenced by outside forces beyond their control, such as China's internal developments and the big-power rivalries, never before in modern history have these countries had as much ability to shape these relations, or their relations with other powers, as they have in the mid-1970s.

7

Implications for U.S. Policy

The development of stable and mutually beneficial relations among nations whose combined population is well in
excess of a billion persons and which control vast natural
resources is of great importance to the United States and to
world peace. Thus it should be U.S. policy to encourage the
development of such relations among the nations of
Southeast Asia and China, bearing in mind at the same time
that the conduct of their foreign relations is their own
responsibility and above all their own right.

As already noted, the trend toward normalization of Sino–
Southeast Asian relations resulted in large part from intensified Sino-Soviet hostility and the partial rapprochement
between Washington and Peking. These and other shifts in
relationships between the United States, the Soviet Union,
the PRC, and Japan in the early 1970s brought about the

present four-power balance in East Asia, perhaps better described as a four-power system.[164] By helping to preserve this system the United States can make a major contribution toward continuing the normalization trend.

The U.S. stake in preserving the four-power system goes well beyond its interest in stable Sino–Southeast Asian relations, of course, and a discussion of policies necessary to preserve it goes beyond the scope of this brief study. Suffice it to say that such policies must involve maintaining a military presence in the Western Pacific sufficiently strong to give credibility to U.S. mutual defense commitments there, as well as preserving a posture of détente toward both the PRC and the Soviet Union.

The four-power system not only represents a balance of forces but also a balance of interests. Each of its members, for example, has an interest in preventing the others from dominating Southeast Asia. Whatever interest one may have in seeking hegemony over the region is balanced by the opposition of the other three. Hegemony, in fact, has become a dirty word in the diplomatic vocabulary of East Asia. Both Peking and Moscow in their propaganda battles describe the other's aims in Southeast Asia as "hegemonistic." President Nixon and Premier Chou En-lai, in their celebrated Shanghai communiqué of February 28, 1972, declared that neither the United States nor the PRC "should seek hegemony in the Asia-Pacific region and each is opposed to efforts by any other country or group of countries to establish such hegemony." Similar sentiments were expressed by the PRC and Japan when they established diplomatic relations in September 1972.

The unanimous opposition to hegemony professed by the members of the four-power system is shared by the countries of Southeast Asia. Big-power hegemony would threaten their independence and freedom of action. The ASEAN foreign ministers gave expression to Southeast Asian fears in their November 1971 proposal for the establishment, and international recognition, of Southeast Asia as a zone of peace, freedom, and neutrality.

Despite everyone's opposition to hegemony and restraints put upon the major powers' exercise of it by the existence of the four-power balance, fears of it persist. These are based on the existence of a so-called power vacuum in Southeast Asia created by U.S. military withdrawal from Indochina and from Thailand. Peking and Moscow accuse each other of trying to fill this vacuum. Similar worries are heard in the United States. In the long run the best protection Southeast Asian countries have against big-power hegemony is to eliminate the power vacuum by building up their own power through regional cooperation.

With ASEAN they have taken a long stride in this direction. While ASEAN is not yet organized to marshal the considerable resources of its five members in their common defense, as a political instrument it has real significance. A purely Southeast Asian product, ASEAN has demonstrated that countries of the region can cooperate effectively in their common interest. A united stand by the ASEAN countries on matters affecting their own security could not be defied with impunity by any power. The so-called power vacuum left by the United States need not be filled by any other power if ASEAN stands firm against such a move. Moreover, to the extent that ASEAN countries can fill the vacuum with their own power they reduce the dangers that Sino-Soviet hostility will engulf the region.

While initiatives towards closer regional cooperation must come from Southeast Asia itself to be effective, the United States should encourage and reinforce such initiatives wherever feasible. The phasing out of SEATO, a product of U.S. initiative, is symbolic of the changing U.S.

role in the region. The responsibility for regional security must rest with the regional countries, and the United States should indicate its desire to relinquish in due time its defense commitments in the region in favor of broader multilateral guarantees. These, in contrast to the Soviet proposal for Asian collective security, should develop from Southeast Asian initiatives.

Besides helping to preserve the four-power balance and supporting Southeast Asian initiatives to strengthen regional cooperation, a third way the United States can contribute to stabilizing Sino–Southeast Asian relations is by pursuing policies that help Southeast Asian countries cope with their economic development problems. The concept that economic assistance from the industrialized countries to the developing countries promotes international peace and security was reaffirmed and given broader meaning by the special session of the U.N. General Assembly on development and international economic cooperation held in September 1975. For example, in the preamble of the resolution adopted by the special session on September 16, the General Assembly recognized that "the accelerating development of developing countries would be a decisive element for the promotion of world peace and security" and "greater cooperation among states in the fields of trade, industry, science and technology as well as in other fields of economic activities . . . would also contribute to strengthening peace and security in the world."[165]

The resolution's recommendations went beyond conventional development assistance programs and dealt also with trade, capital markets, science and technology, the world monetary system, and other areas where cooperation should take place between developed and developing countries in order "to increase the capacities of developing countries, individually and collectively, to pursue their development."

The measures called for by the resolution point the way to the kinds of action the United States can take which will be of greatest assistance to Southeast Asian countries in meeting their basic development needs and should be followed up vigorously.

In the long run, this represents the most effective help the United States can provide Southeast Asian governments in their efforts to cope with insurgency. The United States should not become directly involved in such efforts. Much of the insurgency in Southeast Asia today either results primarily from ethnic and/or religious frictions or depends heavily on disaffected ethnic minorities. Outside involvement only tends to exacerbate sensitive internal racial and religious differences. The United States should thus get out of the counterinsurgency business and stay out of it.

This does not mean, however, that the United States should embargo arms sales to governments trying to cope with insurgency. While these governments must handle their insurgency problems by their own efforts, to deny them access to weapons would put them at a disadvantage in the present situation where large supplies of weapons (many of them American) are potentially available to the insurgents. The sale of weapons to foreign governments usually involves providing instruction in their use, and the United States should provide such instruction when essential. But the line should be drawn against further involvement, such as in the training of Southeast Asian military forces in the tactics of counterinsurgency or in the provision of advisers to such forces. This line was successfully maintained in Burma, where the United States had a military sales program in operation for about a dozen years without becoming involved in counterinsurgency, and it should be adhered to elsewhere.

Normalization of relations between the United States and

the Indo-Chinese countries would help to stabilize relations between the PRC and Southeast Asia, as well as international relations within the region, and should be an objective of U.S. policy.[166] While it may take some time to work out diplomatic relations with all the Indo-Chinese states, the United States should not in the meantime rule out actions to help them meet their development needs. The posture the United States takes towards the Indo-Chinese countries should be forward-looking, rather than backward-looking, and should manifest the desire of the United States to cooperate with them in the spirit of the General Assembly resolution of September 16. Successful implementation of a policy of this kind toward the Indo-Chinese states would depend, of course, on their willingness to adopt a similar stance toward the United States.

Historians may never agree on whether the United States and SEATO actually preserved Southeast Asian independence against a threat from China, as President Kennedy believed, or whether the threat existed only in the American mind. In any case, Communist victory in Indochina has not brought Chinese domination but, ironically, a Chinese perception of a threat of Soviet domination.

As clearly set forth in the ASEAN foreign ministers' proposal of November 1971, Southeast Asians want to conduct their affairs without outside interference. Somewhat paradoxically, this objective can only be achieved with outside cooperation, especially with that of the major powers. The latter must not only live up to their peaceful coexistence and antihegemony professions, but also assist Southeast Asian nations in a positive way to develop their own resources of strength.

Of the major powers, none has a greater stake in the accomplishment of this objective than the PRC. Because of its propinquity, a Southeast Asia composed of peaceful, independent states is more important to China's security than to that of any other major power. Attempts by the PRC to dominate Southeast Asia would be strongly resisted by the countries of the region and would inevitably intensify big-power friction, to the detriment of China's security. The mutual interest that the PRC and Southeast Asian countries have in maintaining Southeast Asian independence reinforces the prospects for the continued normalization of Sino–Southeast Asian relations. But failure of the United States to play its part will jeopardize these prospects and the prospects for peace.

Appendix

Association of Southeast Asian Nations Declaration August 8, 1967, Bangkok

The Presidium Minister for Political Affairs/Minister for Foreign Affairs of Indonesia, the Deputy Prime Minister of Malaysia, the Secretary of Foreign Affairs of the Philippines, the Minister for Foreign Affairs of Singapore and the Minister of Foreign Affairs of Thailand:

Mindful of the existence of mutual interests and common problems among the countries of Southeast Asia and convinced of the need to strengthen further the existing bonds of regional solidarity and cooperation;

Desiring to establish a firm foundation for common action to promote regional cooperation in Southeast Asia in the spirit of equality and partnership and thereby contribute toward peace, progress and prosperity in the region;

Conscious that in an increasingly interdependent world, the cherished ideals of peace, freedom, social justice and economic well-being are best attained by fostering good understanding, good neighbourliness and meaningful cooperation among the countries of the region already bound together by ties of history and culture;

Considering that the countries of Southeast Asia share a primary responsibility for strengthening the economic and social stability of the region and ensuring their peaceful and progressive national development, and that they are determined to ensure their stability and security from external interference in any form or manifestation in order to preserve their national identities in accordance with the ideals and aspirations of their peoples;

Affirming that all foreign bases are temporary and remain only with the expressed concurrence of the countries concerned and are not intended to be used directly or indirectly to subvert the national independence and freedom of states in the area or prejudice the orderly processes of their national development;

Do hereby declare:

First, the establishment of an association for regional cooperation among the countries of Souteast Asia to be known as the Association of Southeast Asian Nations (ASEAN).

Second, that the aims and purposes of the association shall be:

1. to accelerate the economic growth, social progress and cultural development in the region through joint endeavours in the spirit of equality and partnership in order to strengthen the foundation for a prosperous and peaceful community of Southeast Asian nations;

2. to promote regional peace and stability through abiding respect for justice and the rule of law in the relationship among countries of the region and adherence to the principles of the United Nations Charter;

3. to promote active collaboration and mutual assistance on matters of common interest in the economic, social, cultural, technical, scientific and administrative fields;

4. to provide assistance to each other in the form of training and research facilities in the educational, professional, technical and administrative spheres;

5. to collaborate more effectively for the greater utilization of their agriculture and industries, the expansion of their trade, including the study of the problems of international commodity trade, the improvement of their transportation and communication facilities and the raising of the living standards of their peoples;

6. to promote Southeast Asian studies;

7. to maintain close and beneficial cooperation with existing international and regional organizations with similar aims and purposes, and explore all avenues for even closer cooperation among themselves.

Third, that, to carry out these aims and purposes, the

following machinery shall be established:

(a) Annual meeting of Foreign Ministers, which shall be by rotation and referred to as ASEAN Ministerial Meeting. Special meetings of Foreign Ministers may be convened as required.

(b) A Standing Committee, under the chairmanship of the Foreign Minister of the host country or his representative and having as its members the accredited ambassadors of the other member countries, to carry on the work of the Association in between meetings of Foreign Ministers.

(c) Ad Hoc committees and permanent committees of specialists and officials on specific subjects.

(d) A national secretariat in each member country to carry out the work of the Assocation on behalf of that country and to service the annual or special meetings of Foreign Ministers, the Standing Committee and such other committees as may hereafter be established.

Fourth, that the Association is open for participation to all states in the Southeast Asian region subscribing to the aforementioned aims, principles and purposes.

Fifth, that the Association represents the collective will of the nations of Southeast Asia to bind themselves together in friendship and cooperation and, through joint efforts and sacrifices, secure for their peoples and for posterity the blessings of peace, freedom and prosperity.

Done in Bangkok on the eighth day of August in the year one thousand nine hundred and sixty-seven.

Notes

1. Quoted in Senate Foreign Relations Committee, *Background Information Relating to Southeast Asia and Vietnam*, 6th rev. ed. (Washington, D.C.: U.S. Government Printing Office, 1970), p. 204. For similar perceptions of the Chinese threat to Southeast Asia by President Lyndon Johnson and Secretary of State Dean Rusk, respectively, see ibid., p. 225, 250. On the Republican side, Richard Nixon said in "Asia After Viet Nam," *Foreign Affairs*, October 1967: "But now the West has abandoned its colonial role, and it no longer threatens the independence of the Asian nations. Red China, however, does, and its threat is clear, present and repeatedly and insistently expressed."

2. See announcement following SEATO ministerial meeting of September 24, 1975, *New York Times*, September 25, 1975.

3. *New York Times*, February 21, 1976.

4. *Peking Review*, July 4, 1975, p. 11.

5. Albert Feuerwerker, "Chinese History and the Foreign Relations of Contemporary China," *The Annals of the American Academy of Political and Social Science*, July 1972, p. 4.

6. Harold C. Hinton, *China's Turbulent Quest* (Bloomington and London: Indiana University Press, 1972), p. 120. For a similar report of Peking's intentions see David Milton, Nancy Milton, and Franz Schurmann, eds., *The China Reader*, vol. 4 (New York: Random House, 1974), p. 519.

7. John C. Donnell and Melvin Gurtov, "North Vietnam: Left of Moscow, Right of Peking," in Robert A. Scalapino, ed., *The Communist Revolution in Asia* (Englewood Cliffs, N.J.: Prentice-Hall, 1969), p. 163 and n. 30.

8. David Jenkins, "It's a Long Road to Unity," *Far Eastern Economic Review*, February 21, 1975, pp. 31-33.

9. See, for example, Frank N. Trager, "Wars of National Liberation: Implications for U.S. Policy and Planning," *Orbis*, Spring 1974, p. 80.

10. In his well-documented study of Peking's motivations for the use of force, Allen S. Whiting states the Chinese purpose in a slightly different way: "Between 1964 and 1972 the PLA moved upwards of 15,000 troops into the adjacent provinces of Laos to counter parallel covert Thai deployments under American direction." Allen S. Whiting, *The Chinese Calculus of Deterrence* (Ann Arbor: The University of Michigan Press, 1975), p. 236.

11. I was living in Burma during the period and followed these developments closely. The presence of Chinese among the BCP insurgents in eastern Burma became so well known that a friend of mine from that area remarked half-jokingly in the fall of 1973 that soon his compatriots there would be learning Chinese. It was not until early 1974, however, that

reports of Chinese involvement appeared in the American press, by which time the BCP campaign had tapered off. See, for example, the report by Joseph Lelyveld, *New York Times*, February 2, 1974, p. 6, an article in *Time*, March 25, 1974, p. 47, and articles by H. D. S. Greenway and Daniel Southerland in *Washington Post*, April 8, 1974, p. A10 (which also deal with the Chinese military roads in Laos).

12. Though Burma is not mentioned specifically in Chinese media output dealing with this theme, alleged Soviet ambitions in land and sea areas bordering Burma were frequently described and castigated. A good example is the *Peking Review* article, "New Tsars, Old Dream: Social Imperialism's Expansion in South Asia and Indian Ocean," *Peking Review*, December 7, 1973, pp. 15-16.

13. A. Doak Barnett, *Uncertain Passage: China's Transition to the Post-Mao Era* (Washington, D.C.: The Brookings Institution, 1974), p. 248.

14. See Lucian W. Pye, *China: An Introduction* (Boston: Little, Brown and Company, 1972), pp. 300-301.

15. Mao told André Malraux in 1965: "There are two paths for every communist: that of socialist construction and that of revisionism. . . . Even today, broad layers of our society are conditioned in such a way that their activity is necessarily oriented towards revisionism." Quoted in Jerome Chen, ed., *Mao* (Englewood Cliffs, N.J.: Prentice-Hall, 1969), p. 121.

16. William W. Whitson, "Domestic Constraints on Alternative Chinese Military Policies and Strategies in the 1970s," *The Annals of the American Academy of Political and Social Science*, July 1972, p. 49.

17. For a detailed analysis of the makeup of the Central Committees and Politburos elected by the Ninth and Tenth Party Congresses (upon which I have depended here), see Barnett, *Uncertain Passage*, pp. 220-28, 233-39.

18. H. D. S. Greenway, "Region Army Chiefs Reassigned by China," *Washington Post,* January 3, 1974. See also Greenway, "China's Army Reshuffle Seen Political," *Washington Post,* December 24, 1974.

19. H. D. S. Greenway, "China: Signs of a New Campaign," *Washington Post,* December 7, 1974.

20. The text of Chou's report is reproduced in *Peking Review,* January 24, 1975, pp. 21-25.

21. Joseph Lelyveld, "Teng Heads China's Army; 3rd Major Role in Regime," *New York Times,* January 30, 1975.

22. Quoted by Agence France-Presse in *Washington Post,* February 18, 1975.

23. Yao's article is reproduced in *Peking Review,* March 7, 1975, pp. 5-10.

24. As Jack Gray has said, "It is perhaps in the idea of the 'destruction of the three differences' . . . that Mao's point of view on social and economic change is best summed up." Jack Gray, "The Economics of Maoism," in Richard Baum, ed, with Louise B. Bennett, *China in Ferment* (Englewood Cliffs, N.J.: Prentice-Hall, 1971), p. 87.

25. See Fox Butterfield, "Old Chinese Tale, Modern Puzzle," *New York Times,* September 24, 1975; also "Mao Stirs Anti-Book Campaign," September 5, 1975.

26. The editorial is reproduced in *Peking Review,* January 2, 1976, pp. 8-10.

27. Fox Butterfield, "China's Leftists Are Now Called 'Capitalist-Roaders,'" *New York Times,* October 20, 1976.

28. Ross H. Munro, "Chinese Publicize Attack on Minister," *Washington Post,* December 25, 1975.

29. Fox Butterfield, "Education System Debated in China," *New York Times,* December 22, 1975.

30. H. D. S. Greenway, "China Debate: Shades of Berkeley, Columbia in 1960's," *Washington Post,* March 17, 1976.

31. Boyce Rensberger, "Chinese Farm Gains Impress Visitors," *New York Times*, October 7, 1974.

32. Hans Heymann, Jr., "Acquisition and Diffusion of Technology in China," in Joint Economic Committee, *China: A Reassessment of the Economy* (A compendium of papers submitted to the Joint Economic Committee, Congress of the United States, July 10, 1975), p. 705.

33. Ibid., p. 678.

34. Ibid., p. 702.

35. Alva Lewis Erisman, "China: Agriculture in the 1970s," in ibid., p. 349.

36. Heymann, "Acquisition and Diffusion of Technology in China," p. 679.

37. Harry Harding and Melvin Gurtov, *The Purge of Lo Jui-ch'ing: The Politics of Chinese Strategic Planning* (Santa Monica, Calif.: The Rand Corporation, 1971), pp. 52-53.

38. See Sydney H. Jammes, "The Chinese Defense Burden, 1965-74," in *China: A Reassessment*, pp. 463-64.

39. Merle Goldman, "China's Debate Over Priorities," *New York Times*, December 23, 1974.

40. Jammes, "The Chinese Defense Burden," p. 465. The PRC's military expenditures have apparently been increasing since the fall of 1975.

41. Fox Butterfield, "China Combating Factional Strife," *New York Times*, August 19, 1975.

42. "Peking to Go Ahead with Chou Plan for Widespread Modernization," *New York Times*, October 26, 1976.

43. For a similar view on the "doctrine of self-reliance," see Peter Van Ness, *Revolution and Foreign Policy: Peking's Support for Wars of National Liberation* (Berkeley: University of California Press, 1970), p. 112.

44. Indonesia '73 FOCUS, p. 29, in *Far Eastern Economic Review*, December 24, 1973.

45. *Peking Review*, June 7, 1974, p. 9.

46. Teng's remarks on these occasions can be found in *Peking Review*, June 13, 1975, p. 9, and July 4, 1975, p. 9.

47. I heard this comment more than once in private from Burmese officials in 1972-73. The same view has also been expressed by the Indonesian Foreign Minister—see n. 44.

48. The new constitution of the PRC is reproduced in *Peking Review*, January 24, 1975, pp. 12-17.

49. See Barnett, *Uncertain Passage*, p. 246.

50. Quoted by Peter Bathurst, "Common Denominator: Captured Guns," US and Asia FOCUS, p. 8, in *Far Eastern Economic Review*, July 4, 1975. Similar Indonesian concern is reported by Dan Coggin, "Blue-ribbon Verdict on Suharto's Tour," *Far Eastern Economic Review*, August 1, 1975, p. 24.

51. Jeffrey Race, "Thailand in 1974: A New Constitution," *Asian Survey*, February 1975, p. 164. See also "Bad Omens for Troubled Thais," *Far Eastern Economic Review*, August 22, 1975, pp. 10-11, and Lewis M. Simons, "Communist Laos Smuggles Arms into Thailand," *Washington Post*, October 21, 1975.

52. Jay Taylor, *China and Southeast Asia: Peking's Relations with Revolutionary Movements* (New York: Praeger Publishers, 1974), p. 289.

53. "Thailand's Role in Asia," *Far Eastern Economic Review*, December 12, 1975, p. 20.

54. *Peking Review*, December 20, 1974, p. 18.

55. *World Strength of the Communist Party Organizations* (Washington, D.C.: Department of State, July 1973), pp. 96-97.

56. For estimates of Communist insurgent strength in Thailand see Trager, "Wars of National Liberation," pp. 76-77, and Norman Peagam, "The Grass Roots of Rebellion," *Far Eastern Economic Review*, May 9, 1975, p. 27.

57. Lewis M. Simons, "Thai Insurgents, Using Hanoi's Tactics, Step Up Attack," *Washington Post*, April 25, 1975.

58. See Dick Wilson, *The Neutralization of Southeast Asia* (New York, Praeger Publishers, 1975), pp. 126-27. For Hanoi's view, see Nayan Chanda, "ASEAN: Hanoi Says It Again," *Far Eastern Economic Review*, September 10, 1976.

59. Charles B. McLane, *Soviet Strategies in Southeast Asia* (Princeton, N.J.: Princeton University Press, 1966) pp. 383-85.

60. *New York Times*, March 22, 1975. See also M.C. Tun, "A Fatal Mistake for Burma's Communists," *Far Eastern Economic Review*, May 23, 1975, pp. 32, 35.

61. Melvin Gurtov, *China and Southeast Asia—the Politics of Survival: a Study of Foreign Policy Interaction* (Lexington, Mass.: Heath-Lexington Books, 1971), p. 174.

62. *Peking Review*, May 30, 1975, p. 3.

63. C. P. FitzGerald, *China and Southeast Asia Since 1945* (London: Longmans Group Limited, 1973), p. 74.

64. An interesting concrete example is reported by Peter Simms, "The Communist Softsell Falls on Deaf Ears," *Far Eastern Economic Review*, January 24, 1975, p. 20.

65. Taylor, *China and Southeast Asia*, p. 316.

66. *Washington Post*, June 23, 1974.

67. Martin Woollacott, "Malaysia Faces Guerrilla Upsurge," *Washington Post*, November 5, 1975.

68. Leo Goodstadt, "After Détente, Shivers of Apprehension," *Far Eastern Economic Review*, July 11, 1975, p. 24.

69. *Peking Review*, May 2, 1975, p. 6.

70. *World Strength of the Communist Party Organizations*, p. 92.

71. Taylor, *China and Southeast Asia*, p. 309.

72. Ibid., pp. 343-44. An interesting interview with Bong in which he says the NKCP was unable to obtain arms from the PRC appears in *Far Eastern Economic Review*, April 4,

1975, pp. 26-27.

73. Arun Senkutuven, "Puzzling Aftermath of a Security Raid," *Far Eastern Economic Review*, August 15, 1975, p. 11.

74. *World Strength*, pp. 95-96.

75. Ibid., p. 94.

76. Taylor, *China and Southeast Asia*, pp. 326-27.

77. Ibid., p. 329.

78. Bernard Wideman, "Stepping up Terror in Mindanao," *Far Eastern Economic Review*, October 10, 1975, pp. 16-17.

79. *Washington Post*, October 18, 1974.

80. Justis M. van der Kroef, "Guerrilla Communism and Counterinsurgency in Thailand," *Orbis*, Spring 1974, p. 110, n. 12.

81. "The Chinese are Coming," *Far Eastern Economic Review*, October 18, 1974, p. 24.

82. Taylor, *China and Southeast Asia*, p. 82.

83. Guy J. Pauker, "The Rise and Fall of the Communist Party of Indonesia," in Scalapino, ed., *The Communist Revolution in Asia*, p. 299.

84. Taylor, *China and Southeast Asia*, p. 129.

85. Coggin, "Blue-ribbon Verdict on Suharto's Tour," p. 24.

86. Quoted by Harvey Stockwin, "Suharto Meets the Auditors," *Far Esatern Economic Reivew*, March 19, 1973, p. 11. In a magazine interview some months later Foreign Minister Malik commented apropos of the "former PKI leaders": "The Chinese Government already knows our position. We don't like to see that they support these elements. They may support them individually, as human beings, that's alright. But against us, that's finished." See n. 44.

87. K. Das, "A Change in Mood," China '75 FOCUS, p. 28, in *Far Eastern Economic Review*, October 3, 1975.

88. *Peking Review*, May 30, 1975, p. 3.

89. "Still Nervous, and Not So Neutral," Indonesia '75 FOCUS, p. 7, in *Far Eastern Economic Review*, November 7, 1975.

90. See Taylor, *China and Southeast Asia*, p. 201.

91. See Harold C. Hinton, *Communist China in World Politics* (Boston: Houghton Mifflin Co., 1966), pp. 403-5.

92. Stephen FitzGerald, "China and the Overesas Chinese: Perceptions and Policies," *The China Quarterly*, October-December 1970, p. 8.

93. Richard L. Walker, *The Coming Struggle* (New York: Athene Press, Inc., 1958), p. 66.

94. Stephen FitzGerald, "China and the Overseas Chinese," p. 20.

95. C. P. FitzGerald, *China and Southeast Asia Since 1945*, pp. 84-87.

96. Stephen FitzGerald, "China and the Overseas Chinese," p. 21.

97. Proclaimed by Chou En-lai on the occasion of Ne Win's visit to Peking, Taylor, *China and Southeast Asia*, pp. 237-38.

98. "A New Move in the Philippines," *Far Eastern Economic Review*, March 21, 1975, p. 29. Note also C. P. FitzGerald's comment that "in Indonesia, Thailand, and the Philippines the acquisition of local nationality, whether by birth or naturalization, still leaves the Chinese under political and often economic disabilities," in *China and Southeast Asia Since 1945*, p. 92.

99. Brewster Grace, "A Note on Thailand," *Fieldstaff Reports*, (Southeast Asia Series), vol. 22, no. 4, p. 5. An interesting illustration of the phenomenon Grace describes is provided by the Bangkok Bank, which is the subject of Norman Peagam's article, "Southeast Asia's Home-grown Giant," Banking '75 FOCUS, pp. 37-39, in *Far Eastern*

Economic Review, April 25, 1975.

100. See Harvey Stockwin, "The Key Fear," *Far Eastern Economic Review*, October 15, 1973.

101. The text of the joint communiqué can be found in *Peking Review*, June 23, 1974, p. 8. Joint communiqués published by China and the Philippines and China and Thailand approximately a year later affirmed Chinese policy towards Overseas Chinese along similar lines. Texts of these communiqués are contained in *Peking Review*, June 13, 1975, pp. 7-8, and July 4, 1975, pp. 8-9, respectively.

102. Some kind of accord was apparently reached between Kuala Lumpur and Peking for the provision of Chinese travel documents to these stateless Chinese pending a resolution of their status. See M. G. C. Pillai, "Opening the Door to Cooperation," *Far Eastern Economic Review*, May 27, 1974, pp. 27-28.

103. See Harvey Stockwin, "Grasping Chinese Realities," *Far Eastern Economic Review*, October 24, 1975, pp. 16, 19, and Peter Bathurst, "Binding the Minority with Red Tape," May 16, 1975, pp. 40-41.

104. Alexander Eckstein, *Communist China's Economic Growth and Foreign Trade* (New York: McGraw-Hill Book Company, 1966) p. 215. It should be noted that while the author thought Southeast Asia could meet the PRC's basic food and energy deficiencies, he rejected the idea that this prospect might lead Peking to adopt a policy of adventurism in Southeast Asia as some feared.

105. Michael Morrow, "Oil: Catalyst for the Region," *Far Eastern Economic Review*, December 27, 1974, p. 27.

106. Bobby A. Williams, "The Chinese Petroleum Industry: Growth and Prospects," in *China: A Reassessment*, p. 249. The author calculates a production of 226 million tons in 1980 without foreign involvement, with about 50 million tons available for export.

107. Ibid., p. 240.

108. Richard Halloran, "Japan Doubles Oil Purchases from China," *New York Times*, March 11, 1975.

109. Projecting a trade deficit for China of $4.5 billion in 1980, Williams calculates that exports of approximately 35 million tons would cover this deficit with oil at $10 per barrel and exports of just under 30 million tons with oil at $12 per barrel. Williams, "The Chinese Petroleum Industry," p. 248.

110. David A. Andelman, "Thais Reject Chinese Oil as Too Waxy," *New York Times*, September 19, 1975. For a report on the Philippine experience see "The Oil Bonanza Turns Sour," *Far Eastern Economic Review*, November 29, 1974, p. 5. Japanese importers have also experienced trouble with Chinese crude because of its high wax content, as well as its heavy-oil fraction. See Susumu Awanohara, "Snags Facing China's Oil Exports," *Far Eastern Economic Review*, November 28, 1975, pp. 42, 47.

111. Susumu Awanohara "A Contest of Wills," *Far Eastern Economic Review*, May 30, 1975, p. 55.

112. Halloran, "Japan Doubles Oil Purchases."

113. "Indochina: Each to His Own," *Far Eastern Economic Review*, June 13, 1975, p. 25.

114. Although there is no question that China has the world's largest population, just how large it is remains one of the world's mysteries, even to the Chinese themselves. See Leo A. Orleans, "China's Population: Can the Contradictions Be Resolved?" in *China: A Reassessment*, pp. 69-80.

115. Lester R. Brown with Eric Eckholm, *By Bread Alone* (New York: Praeger Publishers, 1974), p. 32.

116. Chou's statement indicates a total grain production of about 260 million tons, i.e., a 140 percent increase over the 108 million tons which was China's grain output for 1949 according to Chinese sources. See Barnett, *Uncertain Pas-*

sage, p. 177, table 4.

117. PRC Vice Minister of Agriculture and Forestry Hao Chung-shih told the United Nations World Food Conference in Rome in November 1974 that for three years China's grain imports and exports had struck "a rough balance in value" of over $2 billion each way. The text of Mr. Hao's speech is reproduced in *Peking Review*, November 15, 1974, pp. 9-12.

118. See n. 31.

119. See n. 117.

120. Quoted by Chou En-lai in his report to the Fourth National People's Congress. A well-informed discussion of the reasons for PRC grain imports is contained in Audrey Donnithorne, *China's Grain: Output, Procurement, Transfers and Trade* (Hong Kong: The Chinese University of Hong Kong, 1970).

121. Carol H. Fogarty, "China's Economic Relations with the Third World," in *China: A Reassessment*, pp. 736-37.

122. Based on statistics in *Direction of Trade*, November 1975 to February 1976.

123. For a discussion of "multilateralism" and the PRC's Southeast Asia trade, see David L. Denny, "International Finance in the People's Republic of China," in *China: A Reassessment*, pp. 656-57.

124. See Eckstein, *Communist China's Economic Growth*, pp. 197-99, and Hinton, *Communist China*, p. 407, for examples.

125. Wolfgang Bartke, *China's Economic Aid* (London: C. Hurst and Company, 1975), p. 36. See also pp. 95-101 for further details on aid to Cambodia.

126. Ibid., p. 49, 126-27.

127. See "Peking to the Rescue," *Far Eastern Economic*

Review, November 1, 1974, p. 38, and "Laos: Filling the Void," *Far Eastern Economic Review*, June 13, 1975, p. 30. The PRC, as might be expected, is continuing to provide economic aid to the new Communist government of Laos. See Fox Butterfield, "Laotians Quit Peking With Pact Assuring China Vientiane Role," *New York Times*, March 20, 1976.

128. Fogarty, "China's Economic Relations with the Third World," p. 734.

129. Bartke, *China's Economic Aid*, p. 12.

130. *Peking Review*, July 4, 1975, p. 12.

131. Edgar Snow, *The Long Revolution* (New York: Random House, 1972), pp. 180-81.

132. Ibid., p. 183.

133. This figure for Soviet troop strength is attributed to Chou En-lai by William E. Griffith, *Peking, Moscow and Beyond* (Washington, D.C.: The Center for Strategic and International Studies, Georgetown University, 1973), p. 13. See also John Burns, "Chinese Leaders, in Policy Change, Play Down Moscow as a Threat," *New York Times*, October 5, 1974.

134. Fox Butterfield, "China Increases Soviet Criticism," *New York Times*, July 11, 1975.

135. "Fighting a New Kind of War," *Far Eastern Economic Review*, September 26, 1975, p. 10. For Moscow's view see Miles Hanley, "A Feeling of Smugness in the Kremlin," *Far Eastern Economic Review*, October 3, 1975, pp. 19-20.

136. Richard Halloran, "Soviet Influence Noted in Saigon," *New York Times*, February 15, 1976.

137. Edith Lenart, "Hanoi's International Stage Setter," *Far Eastern Economic Review*, November 21, 1975, p. 22.

138. Nayan Chanda, "Sino-Soviet Rivalry: Islands of Friction," *Far Eastern Economic Review*, December 12, 1975, pp. 28-29.

139. "Soviet and Hanoi Spur Role in Laos," *New York Times*, June 16, 1975.

140. H. D. S. Greenway, "Pathet Lao Oust King, Government," *Washington Post*, December 4, 1975.

141. "Hanoi and Vientiane Agree on Measures to Strengthen Ties," *New York Times*, February 12, 1976.

142. Ibid.

143. Ross H. Munro, "Cambodia Lines up with China," *Washington Post*, August 20, 1975, p. A18.

144. See Fox Butterfield, "Cambodia Appoints Deputy Ministers," *New York Times*, August 14, 1975.

145. See n. 137.

146. "Laos Replaces U.S. Unit with 1,500 Russians," *New York Times*, August 29, 1975.

147. For a discussion of the Brezhnev proposal, its origins and objectives, and Asian reactions to it, see Alexander Ghebhardt, "The Soviet System of Collective Security in Asia," *Asian Survey*, December 1973, pp. 1075-91; also Arnold L. Horelick, "The Soviet Union's Asian Collective Security Proposal; A Club in Search of Members," *Pacific Affairs*, Fall 1974, pp. 269-85.

148. See *Current Digest of the Soviet Press*, September 5, 1973, p. 10.

149. "Oppose Big Powers Seeking Hegemony," *Peking Review*, April 20, 1973, pp. 13-15.

150. "System for 'Security' or for 'Aggression and Expansion," *Peking Review*, December 28, 1973, pp. 7-9.

151. For a good discussion of Soviet motives see Thomas W. Robinson, "Soviet Policy in East Asia," *Problems of Communism*, November/December 1973, pp. 32-50.

152. The Razak and Malik statements are quoted in Justus M. van der Kroef, "ASEAN's Security Needs and Policies," *Pacific Affairs*, Summer 1974, pp. 160 and 161, respectively.

153. The full text may be found in Wilson, *The Neutralization of Southeast Asia,* pp. 198-99.

154. Christopher S. Wren, "Soviet Bids for Asian Accord," *New York Times,* August 28, 1975.

155. Japan helped to overcome feelings of anti-Japanese prejudice in Southeast Asia by making reparations settlements. These settlements not only had a positive psychological effect but served as entering wedges for Japanese trade and investment. See Donald C. Hellmann, *Japan and East Asia: The New International Order* (New York: Praeger Publishers, 1972), pp. 103-5.

156. Susuma Awanohara, "A Change of Tack," Japan, '75 FOCUS, p. 31, in *Far Eastern Economic Review,* May 23, 1975.

157. For an interesting discussion of such concepts see John K. Emmerson, *Arms, Yen & Power: The Japanese Dilemma* (New York: Dunellen, 1971), pp. 279-84.

158. Saburo Okita spells out the extent of Japan's dependence on foreign resources and its implications in his "National Resources and Japan," *Foreign Affairs,* July 1974, pp. 714-24.

159. Susuma Awanohara, "Japan Prospers at Asia's Expense," *Far Eastern Economic Review,* February 7, 1975, p. 44.

160. Dick Wilson, "Japan Looks at Hanoi for Business," *Far Eastern Economic Review,* May 16, 1975, p. 46.

161. See statement of Japanese Director General of Defense in Emmerson, *Arms, Yen & Power,* p. 307.

162. See n. 12.

163. H. D. S. Greenway, "S.E. Asia Summit to Begin," *Washington Post,* February 23, 1976.

164. For a good discussion of the four-power system see Ralph N. Clough, *East Asia and U.S. Security* (Washington, D.C.: The Brookings Institution, 1975), chapter 3. While the

phrase "four-power balance" which I have used may seem incongruous if thought of in purely military terms, since China and especially Japan are outmatched by the so-called superpowers, it conveys an image of the four-power relationship which I think is valid. A simple analogy might be that of two big boys on either end of a seesaw and two smaller ones positioned in between to balance it. Any radical shift of position by either of the smaller boys would upset the seesaw's balance.

165. "Preamble and Excerpts from U.N. Summary of Development Text," *New York Times*, September 17, 1975.

166. A step in this direction was apparently taken by the U.S. with the delivery of a diplomatic note to the North Vietnamese Embassy in Paris on March 25, 1976. "U.S. Invites Talks with Hanoi, Says It Hopes for Normal Ties," *New York Times*, March 27, 1976.